# SCOTTISH TREASURE TROVE

# SCOTTISH TREASURE TROVE

## Selected and Introduced by George Blake

With a Foreword by
*Russell Hunter*

THE MOLENDINAR PRESS
Glasgow

The Molendinar Press
73 Robertson Street,
Glasgow, Scotland.

© The Estate of George Blake
First published 1928
Reprinted with revisions 1979
ISBN 0904002 30 6

Printed in Great Britain by Waterside Printers.

# FOREWORD

I don't read Forewords; I hope you do. I'm writing this one because I hope you will enjoy this collection made by George Blake fifty years ago — and I think it will have something for readers of all kinds and ages — and you will also go on to read some of the work of one of Scotland's foremost novelists. His novels and essays are well worth reading for themselves as well as being a revealing part of Scottish writing this century.

An idea of George Blake's wit and feeling can be seen in the choice of items in *Scottish Treasure Trove*. At one moment the reader is cajoled and made nostalgic by an extract and on the next page he is faced with the historical reality. What inspired cheek to put the words of Ae Fond Kiss next to Boswell's piece on The Smells of Edinburgh! The book is as unpredictable as a Glasgow drunk, who from being truculent and aggressive changes in the next breath to melodious sentimentality.

My own gleanings from this volume have brought up many revelations, not least a number of unfamiliar writers, as well as rediscovering the familiar in writers like Scott, Burns, Carlyle and Stevenson. My own particular favourite is probably William Power on the singing of Auld Lang Syne, which I shall quote at every Burns Supper for the rest of my life.

*Scottish Treasure Trove* is a book to keep on your bedside table or in your briefcase or handbag, as it can be dipped into and re-read many times. Give it to real friends so that you can share the enjoyment. Never lend it to anyone.

*Russell Hunter 1979*

# PREFACE

THIS volume has been designed as a companion to " Treasure Trove," edited by John o' London, and published in 1925 in this series of John o' London's Little Books. But whereas John o' London ranged the wide world for his " fragments of verse and prose which readers have found to be inspiring or of curious interest," it has been the business of the present compilers—for Mr. George Malcolm Thomson has had a large hand in the affair—to confine themselves to passages affecting Scotland only, passages expressive or critical of Scottish life and sentiment.

" Scottish Treasure Trove " is not an anthology in the proper sense of the word ; considerations of space and copyright have denied it exhaustiveness ; but I think that it is thoroughly representative and that it will give pleasure and entertainment, not only to Scots at home and abroad, but also to all those who take delight in the curiosities of literature and life.

A glossary of the less familiar Scots words will be found at the end of the book.

For permission to reprint from copyright works, grateful acknowledgments are hereby made to Sir James Barrie ; Mr. R. B. Cunninghame Graham and Messrs. Ernest Benn ; Mr. Neil Munro ; Dr. George Saintsbury and Messrs. Macmillan & Co. ; Mr. Logan Pearsall Smith and Messrs. Constable & Co. ; Messrs. Thomas Nelson & Sons, for the fragment from " The House With the Green Shutters " ; Mr. William Power ; Mr. G. K. Chesterton and Messrs. Methuen & Co.; the Reverend Kenneth Macleod ; Mr. Harold William Thompson and the Oxford University Press, for the extracts from Henry Mackenzie's " Anecdotes and Egotisms " ; Mr. John Buchan ; Mr. G. K. Menzies ; Messrs. John Lane, The Bodley Head, for the passage from " The Fugger News Letters " ; Miss Margaret Warrender, for " Annie Laurie," from " Songs and Verses," by Lady John Scott ; and Messrs. Chatto and Windus, for " Blows the Wind To-day," by Robert Louis Stevenson.

G. B.

# SCOTTISH TREASURE TROVE

**"BREATHES THERE THE MAN."**

Breathes there the man with soul so dead,
Who never to himself hath said,
" This is my own, my native land ! "
Whose heart hath ne'er within him burn'd
As home his footsteps he hath turn'd
    From wandering on a foreign strand ?
If such there breathe, go, mark him well ;
For him no Minstrel raptures swell ;
High though his titles, proud his name,
Boundless his wealth as wish can claim ;
Despite those titles, power, and pelf,
The wretch, concentred all in self,
Living, shall forfeit fair renown,
And, doubly dying, shall go down
To the vile dust from whence he sprung,
Unwept, unhonour'd, and unsung.
        *Sir Walter Scott : " Lay of the*
        *Last Minstrel."*

Looked at broadly, one would say they had been an eminently pious people. It is part of the complaint of modern philosophers about them, that religion, or superstition, or whatever they please to call it, had too much to do with their daily lives. So far as one can look into that commonplace round of things which historians never tell us about, there have rarely been seen in this world a set of people who have thought more about right and wrong, and the judgment about them of the upper powers. Long-headed, thrifty industry—a sound hatred of waste, imprudence, idleness, extravagance—the feet planted firmly upon the earth—a conscientious sense that the worldly virtues are, nevertheless, very necessary virtues, that without these, honesty for one thing is not possible, and that without honesty no other excellence, religious or moral, is worth anything at all—this is the stuff of which Scotch life was made, and very good stuff it is. . . . Among other good qualities, the Scots have been distinguished for humour—not for venomous wit, but for kindly, genial humour, which half loves what it laughs at—and this alone shows clearly enough that those to whom it belongs have not looked too exclusively on the gloomy side of the world. I should rather say that the Scots had been an unusually happy people. Intelligent industry, the honest doing of daily work, with a sense that it must be done well, under penalties; the necessaries of life moderately provided for; and a sensible content with the situation of life in which men are born—this through the week, and at the end of it the "Cotter's Saturday Night"—the homely family, gathered reverently and peacefully together, and irradiated with a sacred presence. Happiness! such happiness as we human creatures are likely to know upon this world, will be found there, if anywhere.

*James Anthony Froude : In his Rectorial Address at Edinburgh University.*

♣    ♣    ♣

## THE FLOWERS OF THE FOREST.

The lady who wrote this haunting song of national sorrow was the daughter of Sir Gilbert Elliot of Minto, Lord Justice-clerk of Scotland. She died in 1805. It is said that, following a talk about the disaster at Flodden, Sir Gilbert offered a bet that Miss Jean could not compose a ballad on the subject. How magnificently she pieced together the fragments of a lost ballad may be judged from this reply to the challenge.

I've heard the lilting at our yowe-milking,
    Lasses a-lilting before the dawn of day;

But now they are moaning in ilka green loan-
ing—
 The Flowers of the Forest are a' wede away.
At buchts, in the morning, nae blythe lads are
 scorning,
 The lasses are lonely, and dowie, and wae ;
Nae daffin', nae gabbin', but sighing and
 sabbing,
 Ilk ane lifts her leglen and hies her away.

In hairst, at the shearing, nae youths now are
 jeering,
 The bandsters are lyart, and runkled, and
 gray ;
At fair, or at preaching, nae wooing, nae
 fleeching—
 The Flowers of the Forest are a' wede away.

At e'en, at the gloaming, nae swankies are
 roaming,
 'Bout stacks wi' the lasses at bogle to play ;
But ilk ane sits drearie, lamenting her dearie—
 The Flowers of the Forest are a' wede away.

Dule and wae for the order sent our lads to the
 Border !
 The English, for ance, by guile wan the day ;
The Flowers of the Forest, that focht aye the
 foremost,
 The prime o' our land, are cauld in the clay.

We'll hear nae mair lilting at our yowe-milking,
   Women and bairns are heartless and wae ;
Sighing and moaning on ilka green loaning—
   The Flowers of the Forest are a' wede away.

Jean Elliot.

❧     ❧     ❧

## BURNS AND SCOTT.

The meeting of the boy, Walter Scott, with the established poet, Robert Burns, was one of the great moments of literary history. This is Scott's classic story of the encounter.

I saw him one day at the late venerable Professor Ferguson's, where there were several gentlemen of literary reputation, among whom I remember the celebrated Mr. Dugald Stewart. Of course, we youngsters sat silent, looked and listened. The only thing I remember which was remarkable in Burns's manner, was the effect produced upon him by a print of Bunbury's, representing a soldier lying dead on the snow, his dog sitting in misery on one side—on the other, his widow, with a child in her arms. These lines were written beneath :

" Cold on Canadian hills, or Minden's plain,
   Perhaps that mother wept her soldier slain ;

Bent o'er her babe, her eye dissolved in dew,
The big drops mingling with the milk he
drew
Gave the sad presage of his future years,
The child of misery baptised in tears."

Burns seemed much affected by the print, or
rather by the ideas which it suggested to his
mind. He actually shed tears. He asked whose
the lines were ; and it chanced that nobody but
myself remembered that they occur in a half-
forgotten poem of Langhorne's called by the
unpromising title of " The Justice of Peace."
I whispered my information to a friend present ;
he mentioned it to Burns, who rewarded me a
look and a word, which, though of mere civility,
I then received and still recollect with very
great pleasure.

His person was strong and robust ; his man-
ners rustic, not clownish ; a sort of dignified
plainness and simplicity, which received part of
its effect perhaps from one's knowledge of his
extraordinary talents. His features are repre-
sented in Mr. Nasmyth's picture : but to me it
conveys the idea that they are diminished, as if
seen in perspective. I think his countenance
was more massive than it looks in any of the
portraits. I should have taken the poet, had I
not known what he was, for a very sagacious

country farmer of the old Scotch school, *i.e.*, none of your modern agriculturists who keep labourers for their drudgery, but the *douce gudeman* who held his own plough. There was a strong expression of sense and shrewdness in all his lineaments ; the eye alone, I think, indicated the poetical character and temperament. It was large, and of a dark cast, which glowed (I say literally *glowed*) when he spoke with feeling or interest. I never saw such another eye in a human head, though I have seen the most distinguished men of my time. His conversation expressed perfect self-confidence, without the slightest presumption. Among the men who were the most learned of their time and country, he expressed himself with perfect firmness, but without the least intrusive forwardness ; and when he differed in opinion, he did not hesitate to express it firmly, yet at the same time with modesty. I have only to add, that his dress corresponded with his manner. He was like a farmer dressed in his best to dine with the laird. I do not speak in *malam partem*, when I say, I never saw a man in company with his superiors in station or information more perfectly free from either the reality or the affectation of embarrassment.

*Sir Walter Scott.*

## PROVIDENCE.

This honest verse gave Scotland one proverbial phrase and may be said to express perfectly a typical piece of Scottish philosophy.

Confide ye aye in Providence, for Providence is
    kind,
And bear ye a' life's changes wi' a calm and
    tranquil mind ;
Tho' press'd and hemm'd on ev'ry side, ha'e
    faith and ye'll win through,
For ilka blade o' grass keeps its ain drap o' dew.
James Ballantine.

♣    ♣    ♣

## SCOTS PROVERBS.

A' are guid lasses, but where do a' the ill wives come frae ?

A cock aye craws crousest on his ain midden-head.

A hungry man sees far.

De'il stick pride, for my dog deed o't.

He that gets gear before he gets wit, is but a short time the master o' it.

    The gravest fish is an oyster ;
    The gravest bird is an owl ;
    The gravest beast's an ass ;
    An' the gravest man is a fule.

When the craw flees, her tail follows.

" There's nae place like hame," quoth the de'il, when he found himself in the Court o' Session.

♣    ♣    ♣

## SEA SOUNDS.

The notes by the Rev. Kenneth Macleod to Mrs. Kennedy-Fraser's remarkable " Songs of the Hebrides " are packed with interesting sidelights on the somewhat mysterious mentality of the Highlander. This passage describes, not a poetic fantasy, but a mood that is very much of a reality to those born and brought up within sight and sound of the Atlantic.

The sounds of the western sea are aye such as can be understanded of the folk. They foretell good weather and bad, birth and death in the township, the drowning of dear ones on faraway shores. In the storm they voice the majesty of the King of the Elements, and in the quiet evening they fill one with a longing which is hope born of pain. Perhaps other seas have voices for other folk, but the western sea alone can speak in the Gaelic tongue and reach the Gaelic heart. . . . And if the sea-sounds are sweet to the islesman at home, they are sweeter still when by faith he hears them in the heart of the mainland, with the unfeeling mountains closing him in. . . .

Centuries come and centuries go, but the sea-voices never lose their old charm. A few years ago a young Skyeman working in Glengarry succeeded, by sleight of heart, in glorifying a very tiny waterfall into a mighty sea. " I sit in the heather and close my eyes," he said, " and methinks the waterfall is the western sea—and, O man of my heart, my heaven and my folk are in that music." More wonderful still was the gift of the Lews servant girl in Glasgow, who could hear twelve different sea-sounds in the roar of the electric cars and the street traffic.

*Kenneth Macleod : In his Notes to*
*" Songs of the Hebrides."*

♣ ♣ ♣

## A LAMENT.

This beautiful song is of obscure origin. It has been called " The Marchioness of Douglas's Lament," but it has no proven connection with any historical incident. However that may be, it carries the full weight of the sweet melancholy and haunting sense of doom that are in all Scottish poetry. The reader may even find in the penultimate verse the gist of all the poetry ever written !

O waly, waly, up the bank,
    And waly, waly, doun the brae,
And waly, waly, yon burn-side,
    Where I and my Love wont to gae !

I lean'd my back unto an aik,
  I thocht it was a trustie tree ;
But first it bow'd and syne it brak—
  Sae my true love did lichtlie me.

O waly, waly, but love is bonnie
  A little time while it is new !
But when 'tis auld it waxeth cauld,
  And fades awa' like morning dew.

.      .      .      .      .

Mart' mas wind, when wilt thou blaw,
  And shake the green leaves aff the tree ?
O gentle Death, when wilt thou come ?
  For of my life I am wearie.

'Tis not the frost, that freezes fell,
  Nor blawing snaw's inclemencie,
'Tis not sic cauld that makes me cry ;
  But my Love's heart grown cauld to me.

When we cam' in by Glasgow toun,
  We were a comely sicht to see ;
My Love was clad in the black velvèt,
  And I mysel' in cramasie.

But had I wist, before I kist,
  That love had been sae ill to win,
I had lock'd my heart in a case o' gowd,
  And pinn'd it wi' a siller pin.

And O ! if my young babe were born,
 And set upon the nurse's knee ;
And I mysel' were dead and gane,
 And the green grass growing over me !

  &clubs;  &clubs;  &clubs;

## A LEGAL PEDANT.

Of all the legal portraits in Henry Cockburn's " Memorials of his Time," there is none more pungent and amusing than that of Sir David Rae, Bart., Lord Eskgrove, a fatuous Law Lord of the early nineteenth century. Here we have a grotesque picture of the Scots Tory of the old school, scared to death by the reactions of the French Revolution, expressing himself in violent Doric.

Everything was connected by his terror with Republican horrors. I heard him, in condemning a tailor to death for murdering a soldier by stabbing him, aggravate the offence thus, " and not only did you murder him, whereby he was berea-ved of his life, but you did thrust, or push, or pierce, or project, or propell, the le-thall weapon through the belly-band of his regimental breeches, which were his Majes-ty's ! " . . .

&clubs;

In the trial of Glengarry for murder in a duel, a lady of great beauty was called as a witness. She came into Court veiled. But before administering the oath Eskgrove gave her this exposition of her duty—" Youngg woman ! you will now consider yourself as in the presence of Almighty God, and of this High Court. Lift up your veil; throw off all modesty, and look me in the face." . . .

&

Rae had to condemn two or three persons to die who had broken into a house at Luss, and assaulted Sir James Colquhoun and others, and robbed them of a large sum of money. He first, as was his almost constant practice, explained the nature of the various crimes, assault, robbery, and hamesucken—of which last he gave them the etymology; and he then reminded them that they attacked the house and the persons within it, and robbed them, and then came to this climax—" All this you did; and God preserve us! joost when they were sitten doon to their denner!"

*Henry Cockburn : " Memorials of his Time."*

    ♣    ♣    ♣

PUTTING THE MOUNTAINS IN THEIR PLACES.

We passed through Glensheal, with prodigious mountains on each side. We saw where the battle was fought in the year 1719. Dr. Johnson owned he was now in a scene of as wild nature as he could see; but he corrected me sometimes in my inaccurate observations.—

" There (said I), is a mountain like a cone,"—
JOHNSON : " No, sir. It would be called so in
a book ; and when a man comes to look at it,
he sees it is not so. It is indeed pointed at
the top ; but one side of it is larger than the
other."—Another mountain I called immense.
—JOHNSON : " No ; it is no more than a considerable protuberance."

> *James Boswell : " Journal of a Tour
> to the Hebrides."*

❧    ❧    ❧

## PLEASANT POISON.

The spirit drunk in the North is drawn from
barley. I never tasted it, except once for experi-
ment at the inn in Inveraray, when I thought it
preferable to any English malt brandy. It was
strong, but not pungent, and was free from the
empyreumatic taste or smell. What was the
process I had no opportunity of inquiring, nor
do I wish to improve the art of making poison
pleasant.

> *Samuel Johnson : " Journey to the
> Western Islands."*

❧    ❧    ❧

## " MY NAME IS NORVAL."

These four lines are all that remain in the popular memory
of John Home's ambitious tragedy, " Douglas." Yet it

was on the first production of the piece that an excited Scotsman cried to the world his rousing question : " Whaur's yer Wullie Shakespeare noo ? "

My name is Norval ; on the Grampian hills
My father feeds his flocks ; a frugal swain,
Whose constant cares were to increase his store,
And keep his only son, myself, at home.
*John Home : " Douglas."*

Not that Scotland was unanimous as to the merits of the play. Here is a contemporary comment on the once-famous tragedy :—

When Garrick had a' *Douglas* read,
He glowered with baith his een ;
And stamping with his foot, he said,
Sic damned stuff ne'er was seen.

♣      ♣      ♣

## WHO MADE AMERICA ?

Who made the American nation ? A little more than a century ago, what was the American ? A puny, miserable colonist, a dependent of another nation. He was nothing higher, nothing better, than a Canadian—a man without a country, and therefore, but little of a man. Who gave the American a country ? Bancroft tells : " The first voice for dissolving all connection with Great Britain came not from the Puritans of New England, the Dutch of New

York, or the planters of Virginia, but from the Scotch Presbyterians of North Carolina."

*Andrew Carnegie, in a Speech to the New York St. Andrew's Society*, 1891.

&#9827;  &#9827;  &#9827;

## ICHTHYOLOGY AND PIETY.

This preposterous catalogue of the sea's riches was compiled, in the sincerest devotional spirit, by Zachary Boyd (1585–1653), Minister of the Barony, Glasgow, and thrice Rector of Glasgow University.

God's might so peopled hath the sea
 With fish of divers sort,
That men therein may clearly see
 Great things for their comfort.

There is such a great varietie,
 Of fishes of all kind,
That it were great impiete
 God's hand there not to find.

The Puffen Torteuse and Thorneback,
 The Scillop and the Goujeon,
The Shrimpe, the Spit-fish, and the Sprat,
 The Stock-fish, and the Sturgeon ;

The Torteuse, Tench, and Tunnyfish,
 The Sparling and the Trout ;
And Herring for the poor man's dish,
 Is all the land about ;

24

The Groundling, Gilt-head, and the Crab,
  The Gurnard, Cockle, Oyster,
The Cramp-fish and als the Sea-Dog,
  The Crefish and the Conger ;
The Periwinkle and Twinfish—
  It's hard to count them all ;
Some are for oyle, some for the dish ;
  The greatest is the Whale !

                              *Zachary Boyd.*

♣      ♣      ♣

### IN THE DAYS OF MIGHTY DRINKERS.

Lord Glenorchy, who was rather fond of his
bottle, gave a very sensible direction to his servant, if he dined out of a Sunday and had
exceeded a little in drinking with the company.
Lady Glenorchy, who was a very pious woman,
went generally on Sunday evenings to a religious
meeting at the house of Dr. Walker, minister
of the High Church, and Lord Glenorchy used
to attend.  But if he was to dine in company, he
told his servant, when he came to attend him to
his carriage, to offer him the wrong side of his
surtout, and if he objected to it, to carry him to
the meeting ;  if he tried to put it on as it was,
to carry him home.

          *Henry Mackenzie :  " Anecdotes and
          Egotisms."*

## AN EPITAPH.

Hislop quotes this epitaph in his " Book of Scottish Anecdote " but does not indicate its source. It is, however, even if apocryphal, so deliciously direct that it deserves to be quoted as a characteristic flower of the grimmer sort of Scots humour.

Here lies interr'd a man o' micht,
  They ca'd him Malcolm Downie ;
He lost his life ae market nicht,
  By fa'ing aff his pownie.
    Aged 37 years.

🦚    🦚    🦚

## SCOTLAND'S FIRST ZOO.

At this tyme, thair wes brocht to this natioun ane heigh great beast, callit ane Drummodrary, quhilk being keipit clos in the Cannogait, nane hade a sight of it without thrie pence the persone, quhilk producit much gayne to the keipar. . . . Thair wes brocht in with it ane lytill baboun, faced lyke unto a naip.

  *John Nicoll* (1590—1667) *: " Diary."*

🦚    🦚    🦚

## A RIDDLE.

The answer to this engaging trifle is, of course, " a cherry.'

Come a riddle, come a riddle,
  Come a rot-tot-tot—
A wee, wee man
  Wi' a red, red coat :

26

A staff in his hand
A stane in his throat—
Come a riddle, come a riddle,
Come a rot-tot-tot.

*Traditional.*

♣    ♣    ♣

## THE FLYING LADY.

I am weel assured that the Countess of Dumfreice, Stair's daughter, was under a very odd kind of distemper, and did frequently fly from the one end of the room to the other, and from the one side of the garden to the other; whither by the effects of witchcraft upon her, or some other way, is a secret. The matter of fact is certain.

*Robert Wodrow (1679—1734)* : *" Memoirs."*

♣    ♣    ♣

## THE ANNUITY.

The Scot can sometimes make fun of the racial infirmities. These lively verses are from a long poem by George Outram, a former editor of the *Glasgow Herald.*

I gaed to spend a week in Fife—
An unco week it proved to be—
For there I met a waesome wife
Lamentin' her viduity.

Her grief brak out sae fierce and fell,
I thought her heart wad burst the shell ;
And—I was sae left to mysel'—
I sell't her an annuity.

The bargain lookit fair enough—
   She just was turned o' saxty-three ;
I couldna guessed she'd prove sae teugh,
   By human ingenuity.
But years have come, and years have gane,
And there she's yet as stieve's a stane—
The limmer's growin' young again,
   Since she got her annuity.

She's crined awa' to bane an' skin,
   But that it seems is nought to me ;
She's like to live—although she's in
   The last stage o' tenuity.
She munches wi' her wizened gums,
An' stumps about on legs o' thrums,
But comes—as sure as Christmas comes—
   To ca' for her annuity.

   .     .     .     .     .

I read the tables drawn wi' care
   For an Insurance Company ;
Her chance o' life was stated there,
   Wi' perfect perspicuity.

But tables here or tables there,
She's lived ten years beyond her share,
An's like to live a dizzen mair,
    To ca' for her annuity.

.      .      .      .      .

Last Yule she had a fearfu' hoast—
    I thought a kink might set me free ;
I led her out, 'mang snaw and frost,
    Wi' constant assiduity.
But Deil ma' care—the blast gaed by,
And missed the auld anatomy ;
It just cost me a tooth, forbye
    Discharging her annuity.

.      .      .      .

The Bible says the age o' man
    Three score an' ten perchance may be
She's ninety-four ;—let them wha can
    Explain the incongruity.
She should hae lived afore the Flood—
She's come o' Patriarchal blood—
She's some auld Pagan, mummified
    Alive for her annuity.

.      .      .      .      .

The water-drap wears out the rock
    As this eternal jaud wears me ;
I could withstand the single shock,
    But no the continuity.

It's pay me here—an' pay me there—
An' pay me, pay me, evermair ;
I'll gang demented wi' despair—
    I'm *charged* for her annuity !
                          *George Outram.*


❧        ❧        ❧


## FRECKLED PRINCE CHARLIE.

This description of Charles Edward Stuart is taken from the " Autobiography " of Alexander Carlyle, the famous Edinburgh divine, who as a boy saw the Prince during his stay at Holyrood after the Battle of Prestonpans :—

I went twice down to the Abbey Court with my friend about twelve o'clock, to wait till the Prince should come out of the Palace and mount his horse to ride to the east side of Arthur Seat to visit his army. I had the good fortune to see him both days, one of which I was close by him when he walked through the guard. He was a good-looking man, of about five feet ten inches ; his hair was dark red, and his eyes black. His features were regular, his visage long, much sunburnt and freckled, and his countenance thoughtful and melancholy. He mounted his horse and rode off through St. Ann's Yards and the Duke's Walk to his army.
                    *Alexander Carlyle : " Autobiography."*

## " SOUND, SOUND THE CLARION ! "

This wonderful verse, which gave the world a proverbial phrase, was long attributed to Scott, who certainly adopted it for his own purposes. It is now recognised as having been written in the body of an otherwise undistinguished poem by one, Major Mordaunt.

Sound, sound the clarion, fill the fife !
To all the sensual world proclaim,
One crowded hour of glorious life
Is worth an age without a name.

*Major Mordaunt.*

♣     ♣     ♣

## THE STIRRUP-CUP.

It has been left to Sir Harry Lauder to make one Gaelic phrase famous throughout the world. Scott long ago explained it thus in " Waverley "—where he cites a special case :—

When the landlord of an inn presented his guests with *deoch an doruis*, that is, the drink at the door, or the stirrup-cup, the draught was not charged in the reckoning. On this point a learned bailie of the town of Forfar pronounced a very sound judgment.

A., an ale-wife in Forfar, had brewed her " peck of malt," and set the liquor out-of-doors to cool ; the cow of B., a neighbour of A., chanced to come by, and seeing the good beverage, was allured to taste it, and finally to drink it up. When A. came to take in her liquor, she found her tub empty, and from the cow's staggering and staring, so as to betray her intemperance, she easily divined the mode in which her "browst" had disappeared. To take vengeance on Crummie's ribs with a stick was her first effort. The roaring of the cow brought B., her master, who remonstrated with his angry neighbour, and received in reply a demand for the value of the ale which Crummie had drunk up. B. refused payment, and was conveyed before C. the bailie, or sitting magistrate. He heard the case patiently ; and then demanded of the plantiff A., whether the cow had sat down to her potation, or taken it standing ? The plaintiff answered, she had not seen the deed committed, but she supposed the cow drank the ale while standing on her feet ; adding, that had she been near she would have made her use them to some purpose. The bailie, on this admission, solemnly adjudged the cow's drink to be *deoch an doruis*—a stirrup-cup, for which no charge could be made, without violating the ancient hospitality of Scotland.

*Sir Walter Scott : " Waverley."*

♣      ♣      ♣

## THE LAIRD'S PRAYER.

Robert Chambers quotes this verse as the rueful litany of a Perthshire gentleman, Maxton of Cultoquey, whose family had suffered considerably at the hands of powerful neighbours: "Wind," in the last line, signifies "boast-fulness."

From the greed of the Campbells,
From the ire of the Drummonds,
From the pride of the Grahams,
From the wind of the Murrays,
Good Lord, deliver us !

♣      ♣      ♣

## A STRANGE DEFINITION.

The humour of this passage from John Jamieson's "Dissertation on the Origin of the Scottish Language" is somewhat obvious, but the old parson's use of doric phrases is delightfully effective. It was bound to interest Jamieson the lexicographer of Braid Scots.

Tradition tells of an old minister in our own country, not of the brightest parts it may be supposed, who, in discoursing from some text in which the word "follow" occurred, informed his audience that he would speak of four different kinds of followers.

"First," said he, "my friends, there are followers ahint ; secondly, there are followers afore ; thirdly, there are followers cheekie for chow, and sidie by sidie ; and last o' a', there are followers that stand stane-still."

*John Jamieson : " Dissertation."*

## TWO RIVERS.

Says Tweed to Till—
" What gars ye rin sae still ? "
Says Till to Tweed—
" Though ye rin with speed
And I rin slaw,
For ae man that ye droon
I droon twa."

*Old Rhyme.*

♣　　♣　　♣

## GOLF IN THE EIGHTEENTH CENTURY.

A very interesting picture of contemporary Scotland is embodied in Smollett's "Humphry Clinker." The book from which the passage is quoted was written, be it remembered, in 1770.

Hard by, in the fields called the Links, the citizens of Edinburgh divert themselves at a game called Golf, in which they use a curious kind of bats, tipped with horn, and small elastic balls of leather, stuffed with feathers, rather less than tennis-balls, but of a much harder consistence ; this they strike with such force and dexterity from one hole to another, that they will fly to an incredible distance. Of this diversion the Scots are so fond, that, when the weather will permit, you may see a multitude of all ranks, from the senator of justice to the lowest tradesman, mingled together in their shirts, and following the balls with the utmost eagerness. Among others, I was shown one particular set of golfers, the youngest of whom was turned of fourscore ; they were all gentlemen of independent fortunes, who had amused themselves with this pastime for the best part of a century, without ever having felt the least alarm from sickness or disgust ; and they never went to bed without having each the best part of a gallon of claret in his belly.

*Tobias Smollett : " Humphry Clinker."*

♣      ♣      ♣

## A TAX ON CLARET.

The imposition of a tax on claret in the eighteenth century grievously offended Scots of the old tradition. These indignant lines were written by one who notoriously loved claret and detested port—John Home, the author of the tragedy, "Douglas," referred to on another page.

Firm and erect the Caledonian stood,
Old was his mutton, and his claret good ;
" Let him drink port," an English statesman
    cried ;
He drank the poison, and his spirit died.

*John Home.*

♣      ♣      ♣

## GENEALOGY.

Scots of the older generation have a passion for genealogical exactitude. It is amusingly illustrated in this

35

passage, quoted by Hislop in his "Book of Scottish Anecdotes."

And so ye see, auld Pittoddles, when his third wife de'ed, he got married upon the laird o' Blaithershins' aughteenth daughter, that was sister to Jemima, that was married until Tam Flumexer, that was first and second cousin to the Pittoddleses, whase brither became laird afterwards, and married Blaithershins' Baubie— and that way Jemima became in a kind o' way her ain niece and her ain aunty, an', as we used to say, her gude-brither was married to his ain grannie.

♣ ♣ ♣

## GOOD OMENS.

West wind to the bairn
    When ga'an for its name ;
And rain to the corpse
    Carried to its lang hame.

A bonny blue sky
    To welcome the bride,
As she gangs to the kirk
    Wi' the sun on her side.

*Traditional.*

## THE GROANING BOARD.

Tobias Smollett was a romanticist, but we may take it that this passage from "Humphry Clinker" fairly describes a ceremonial Scots breakfast in the old days. The occasion of this feast was a funeral.

The following articles formed our morning's repast : one kit of boiled eggs ; a second, full of butter ; a third, full of cream ; an entire cheese, made of goats' milk ; a large earthern pot full of honey ; the best part of a ham ; a cold venison pasty ; a bushel of oatmeal, made in thin cakes and bannocks, with a small wheaten loaf in the middle for the strangers ; a large stone bottle full of whisky, another of brandy, and a kilderkin of ale. There was a ladle chained to the cream kit, with curious wooden bickers to be filled from this reservoir. The spirits were drunk out of a silver quaff, and the ale out of horns. Great justice was done to the collation by the guests in general ; one of them, in particular, ate above two dozen of hard eggs, with a proportionable quantity of bread, butter, and honey ; nor was one drop of liquor left upon the board. Finally, a large roll of tobacco was presented by way of dessert, and every individual took a comfortable quid, to prevent the bad effects of the morning air.

*Tobias Smollett : " Humphry Clinker."*

## LEST THEY BLASPHEMED.

There was a time, not so very long ago, when it was regarded as sacriligious for church choirs in Scotland to rehearse the metrical Psalms to the actual words. For choir-practice, therefore, a number of " dummy " verses, so to speak, were devised. The following examples suggest that these substitute stanzas had a cautiousness all their own :—

> The high, high notes o' Bangor's tune
>     Are very hard to raise ;
> And trying hard to reach them gars
>     The lassies burst their stays.

Another runs thus :—

> I wish I was a brewer's horse
>     Three-quarters of the year ;
> I'd turn my heid where tail should be
>     And drink up all the beer.

And again :—

> I gaed and keekit up the lum
>     The skies for to behold ;
> A daud o' soot fell in my e'e,
>     Which did me quite blindfold.

♣          ♣          ♣

## A PATRIOT IN EXILE.

This notice appeared in the *Scots Magazine*, under the date, August 18th, 1790.

Died at London, Mr. John Stalker, of the Half-moon public-house, Piccadilly. He was a native of Scotland, which he left at an early period. To a life of many oddities, he, dying, exhibited a remarkable instance of the *amor patriæ*, which is the characteristic of his countrymen, being, by express desire, buried in a full suit of the Highland uniform, excepting the *plaid*, which is reserved for his wife's winding-sheet.

♣ ♣ ♣

### "JENNY KISS'D ME."

This pretty little trifle by Leigh Hunt must have a place in a Scots collection, for the Jenny thus celebrated was none other than Jane Welsh Carlyle.

Jenny kiss'd me when we met,
　　Jumping from the chair she sat in ;
Time, you thief, who love to get
　　Sweets into your list, put that in !
Say I'm weary, say I'm sad,
　　Say that health and wealth have miss'd me,
Say I'm growing old, but add,
　　Jenny kiss'd me.

*Leigh Hunt.*

♣ ♣ ♣

### FOR POSTERITY.

" Jock, when ye hae naething else to do, ye may aye be sticking in a tree ; it will be growing, Jock, when ye're sleeping."

*Sir Walter Scott : " The Heart of Midlothian."*

## "FAR ABOVE RUBIES."

This inscription from a stone in Hoddam Churchyard, carries posthumous appreciation to its limit, and amusingly illustrates the traditional Scots affection for Scriptural references.

To the memory of Mary Clow, etc.,
A vertuous wife, a loving mother,
And one esteemed by all who knew her,
And to be short, to her praise, she was
the woman Solomon speaks of in the
xxxi. chapter of the Book of Proverbs,
from the 10th verse to the end.

♣    ♣    ♣

## TO THOSE ABOUT TO MARRY—

It is doubtful if there is in Scottish fiction a finer portrait of a lady of the old school than John Galt's rendering of Leddy Grippy in " The Entail." This is a typical specimen of her worldly wisdom, so shrewdly expressed.

" Gudeman, ye should learn to keep your temper, and be of a composed spirit, and talk wi' me in a sedate manner, when our bairns are changing their life. Watty, my lad, mind what your mother says—' Marriage is a creel, where ye maun catch,' as the auld byword runs, ' an adder or an eel.' But, as I was rehearsing, I could na hae thought that Betty Bodle would hae fa'en just at ance into your grip ; for I had a notion that she was oure souple in the tail to be easily catched. But it's the Lord's will,

Watty ; and I hope ye'll enjoy a' manner o' happiness wi' her, and be a comfort to ane anither, like your father and me,—bringing up your bairns in the fear o' God, as we hae done you, setting them, in your walk and conversation, a pattern of sobriety and honesty, till they come to years of discretion, when, if it's ordained for them, nae doubt, they'll look, as ye hae done, for a settlement in the world, and ye maun part wi' them, as we are obligated, by course of nature, to part with you."

*John Galt : " The Entail."*

♣     ♣     ♣

**IN EXILE.**

The Scot abroad has expressed his nostalgia in many a moving verse. Nothing of the kind is more perfect than this poem, written by Stevenson from the South Seas to S. R. Crockett, who had dedicated to him his book, " The Stickit Minister."

Blows the wind to-day, and the sun and the rain
    are flying,
  Blows the wind on the moors to-day and
    now,
Where about the graves of the martyrs the
    whaups are crying,
  My heart remembers how !

Grey recumbent tombs of the dead in desert
    places,

Standing stones on the vacant wine-red
moor,
Hills of sheep, and the howes of the silent
vanquished races,
And winds, austere and pure ;

Be it granted me to behold you again in
dying,
Hills of home ! and to hear again the call ;
Hear about the graves of the martyrs the pee-
wees crying,
And hear no more at all.

*R. L. Stevenson.*

♣　　♣　　♣

## TO EXILES.

Neil Munro's fine poem is the perfect complement to
Stevenson's cry of homesickness.

Are you not weary in your distant places,
Far, far from Scotland of the mist and storm,
In drowsy airs, the sun-smite on your faces,
The days so long and warm ?
When all around you lie the strange fields
sleeping,
The dreary woods where no fond memories
roam,
Do not your sad hearts over seas come leaping
To the highlands and the lowlands of your
Home ?

Wild cries the Winter, loud through all our
    valleys
    The midnights roar, the grey noons echo back ;
About the scalloped coasts the eager galleys
    Beat for kind harbours from horizons black :
We tread the miry roads, the rain-drenched
    heather,
    We are the men, we battle, we endure !
God's pity for you people in your weather
    Of swooning winds, calm seas, and skies
    demure !

.         .         .         .         .

Let torrents pour then, let the great winds rally,
    Snow-silence fall, or lightning blast the pine ;
That light of Home shines warmly in the valley,
    And, exiled son of Scotland, it is thine.
Far have you wandered over seas of longing,
    And now you drowse, and now you well may
    weep,
When all the recollections come a-thronging
    Of this old country where your fathers sleep.

They sleep, but still the hearth is warmly
    glowing,
    While the wild Winter blusters round their
    land :
That light of Home, the wind so bitter blow-
    ing—

Look, look and listen, do you understand ?
Love, strength, and tempest—oh, come back
    and share them !
Here is the cottage, here the open door ;
Fond are our hearts although we do not bare
    them,
They're yours, and you are ours for evermore.
                    *Neil Munro.*

      ♣      ♣      ♣

## LADY GRIPPY ON THE MODERN GIRL. .

" Lassie, lassie ! " exclaimed the Leddy, " if ye live to be a grandmother like me, ye'll ken the right sense o' a lawful and tender affection. But there's no sincerity noo like the auld sincerity, when me and your honest grandfather, that was in mine, and is noo in Abraham's bosom, came thegither—we had no foistring and parleyvooing, like your novelle turtle-doves— but discoursed in a sober and wise-like manner anent the cost and charge o' a family ; and the upshot was a visibility of solid cordiality and kindness, very different, Beenie, my dear, frae the puff-paste love o' your Clarissy Harlots."

                *John Galt : " The Entail."*

      ♣      ♣      ♣

## " THE AULD MEAR'S DEAD."

This curious and oddly characteristic example of Scots humour in the rueful vein is believed to be the work of

Patrick Birnie, a blind fiddler who flourished in Fifeshire in the eighteenth century. No glossary can deal adequately with the veterinary details in the third verse.

> The auld man's mear's dead ;
> The puir body's mear's dead ;
> The auld man's mear's dead,
>   A mile aboon Dundee.
>
> There was hay to ca', and lint to lead,
> A hunder hotts o' muck to spread,
> And peats and truffs and a' to lead—
>   And yet the jaud to dee !
>
> She had the fiercie and the fleuk,
> The wheezloch and the wanton yeuk ;
> On ilka knee she had a breuk—
>   What ail'd the beast to dee ?
>
> She was lang-tooth'd and blench-lippit,
> Heam-hough'd and haggis-fittit,
> Lang-neckit, chandler-chaftit,
>   And yet the jaud to dee !

♣　　♣　　♣

## HEATHER JOCK.

There are many Scots still living who will remember the original of this brilliant portrait of a " character " once notorious in the West Country.

What reasons influenced William Brodie, bred a weaver at the Bridge of Weir, in Renfrewshire, to first turn pedlar, or, as we say (Scoticé),

" travelling merchant," and from that to trans-
migrate himself into a wandering singer and
buffoon under the name of Heather Jock, are
quite unknown. . . .

No one asked his reasons, but accepted him
just as he was, with headdress like an Inca of
Peru stuck all about with pheasants' and peacock's feathers, bits of looking-glass, adorned
with heather, and fastened underneath his jaws
with a black ribbon ; with moleskin waistcoat ;
bee in his bonnet ; humour in his brain ; with
short plaid trousers, duffel coat, and in his hand
a rude Caduceus made of a hazel stick, and in
the centre a flat tin heart, set round with jingling
bells, and terminating in a tuft of ling. In
figure not unlike a stunted oak of the kind
depicted in the arms of Glasgow, or such as
those which grow in Cadzow Forest, and under
which the white wild cattle feed, as they had
done since Malcolm Fleeming slew one with his
spear and saved the king.

His minstrelsy, if I remember right, was not
extensive as to repertory, being comprised of
but one dreary song about a certain " Annie
Laurie," originally of a sentimental cast, but
which he sang with humorsome effects of face,
at breakneck speed, jangling his bells and jumping about from side to side just like a Texan

cowboy in Sherman, Dallas, or some Pan Handle town during the process of a bar-room fight, to dodge the bullets. At the end he signified his wish to lay him down to die for the object of his song, and did so, elevating, after the fashion of expiring folk, his feet into the air and wagging to and fro his boots adorned with what the Scotch call " tackets."

*R. B. Cunninghame Graham.*

❧    ❧    ❧

## " THE BAIRNIES CUDDLE DOON."

Two verses are sufficient to indicate the sentiment and quality of a poem very popular among the people of Scotland. It was written by Alexander Anderson of Kirkconnel, " Surfaceman," who rose from the rank of railway worker to be Librarian of Edinburgh University.

The bairnies cuddle doon at nicht
   Wi' muckle faught an' din ;
" Oh try and sleep, ye waukrife rogues
   Your faither's comin' in."
They never heed a word I speak :
   I try to gie a froon,
But aye I hap them up an' cry,
   " Oh, bairnies, cuddle doon."

.    .    .    .    .

The bairnies cuddle doon at nicht
   Wi' mirth that's dear to me ;
But soon the big warl's cark an' care
   Will quaten doon their glee.

Yet, come what will to ilka ane,
　　May He wha rules aboon
Aye whisper, though their pows be bald,
　" Oh, bairnies, cuddle doon."
*Alexander Anderson.*

♣　　　♣　　　♣

## " AULD REEKIE."

It was a patriarchial Fife laird, Durham of
Largo, who had the honour of giving to Edinburgh the *sobriquet* of " Auld Reekie."　It
appears that this old gentleman was in the
habit of regulating the time of evening worship
by the appearance of the smoke of Edinburgh,
which he could easily see through the clear
summer twilight from his own door.　When he
observed the smoke increase in density, in con-
sequence of the good folks of the capital pre-
paring their supper, he would call all the family
into the house, saying—

" It's time, noo, bairns to tak the buiks, and
gang to our beds, for yonder's Auld Reekie, I
see, putting on her nichtcap."
*Robert Chambers.*

♣　　　♣　　　♣

## THE CANADIAN BOAT SONG.

The authorship of these lovely verses is still the subject
of lively debate.　They have been attributed to " Christo-

pher North," to John Galt, to Hugh, Earl of Eglinton, and to Scott's son-in-law, John Gibson Lockhart. Another claim has recently been made for one "Tiger" Dunlop. The present compiler prefers not to indicate a preference among these imposing names. It is enough that the beautiful song expresses an essentially Scottish emotion. This famous poem, by the way, is frequently misquoted; the accompanying version is believed to be correct.

Listen to me, as when ye heard our father
Sing long ago the song of other shores—
Listen to me, and then in chorus gather
  All your deep voices, as ye pull your oars:


*Chorus :*
*Fair these broad meads—these hoary woods*
  *are grand,*
*But we are exiles from our fathers' land.*


From the lone shieling of the misty island
  Mountains divide us, and the waste of seas—
Yet still the blood is strong, the heart is Highland,
    land,
  And we in dreams behold the Hebrides.


We ne'er shall tread the fancy-haunted valley,
  Where 'tween the dark hills creeps the small,
    clear stream,
In arms around the patriarch banner rally,
  Nor see the moon on royal tombstones gleam.

When the bold kindred, in the time long-
    vanished,
  Conquer'd the soil and fortified the keep,—
No seer foretold the children would be banish'd,
  That a degenerate Lord might boast his sheep.

Come foreign rage — let Discord burst in
    slaughter !
  O then for clansmen true, and stern clay-
    more—
The hearts that would have given the blood like
    water,
  Beat heavily beyond the Atlantic roar.

*Author unknown.*

&#10070;    &#10070;    &#10070;

## SCOTLAND'S HANGING JUDGE.

Lord Braxfield, the original of Stevenson's "Weir of
Hermiston," was the most terrible personage that ever sat
on the Scottish bench. A hundred legends have gathered
round his name, and some of them are obviously apocryphal,
but contemporary records make it clear enough that he was
a man in whom the coarseness of the North was present in
quintessential strength.

. . . He was the Jeffreys of Scotland. He, as
the head of the Court, and the only very powerful man it contained, was the real director of its
proceedings. The reports make his abuse of
the judgment seat bad enough ; but his mis-

conduct was not so fully disclosed in formal decisions and charges, as it transpired in casual remarks and general manner. " Let them bring me prisoners, and I'll find them law," used to be openly stated as his suggestion, when an intended political prosecution was marred by anticipated difficulties. . . . Mr. Horner (the father of Francis), who was one of the jurors in Muir's case, told me that when he was passing, as was often done then, behind the bench to get into the box, Braxfield, who knew him, whispered—" Come awa, Maister Horner, come awa, and help us to hang ane o' thae daamned scoondrels." The reporter of Gerald's case could not venture to make the prisoner say more than that " Christianity was an innovation " (*State Trials*, Vol. XXIII., p. 972). But the full truth is, that in stating this view he added that all great men had been reformers, " even our Saviour himself." " Muckle he made o' that," chuckled Braxfield in an undervoice, " he was hanget." Before Hume's *Commentaries* had made our criminal record intelligible, the forms and precedents were a mystery understood by the initiated alone, and by nobody so much as by Mr. Joseph Norris, the ancient clerk. Braxfield used to quash anticipated doubts by saying, " Hoot ! just gie me Josie

Norrie and a gude jury and I'll do for the fallow."

> Henry Cockburn : " Memorials of his Time."

♣     ♣     ♣

**OBITER DICTA OF LORD BRAXFIELD.**

Hang a thief when he's young, and he'll no steal when he's auld.

♣

Ye're a vera clever chiel, man ; but ye wad be nane the waur o' a hangin'.

♣

" Lord ! " he exclaimed, to a butler who complained of his lordship's wife's manner towards servants, " ye've little to complain o' ; ye may be thankfu' ye're no married to her."

♣

At a trial, just as the counsel for the prisoner was about to open his address, Lord Braxfield, who was presiding, muttered, loud enough to be heard by a considerable part of the court,

" Ye may spare your pains ; we've determined to hang the —— at ony rate."

## THE SAILOR'S RETURN.

The authorship of this vivid and touching ballad—a perfect expression of Scots domestic sentiment—is disputed. It is sometimes attributed to William Julius Mickle, translator of the *Lusiad ;* a copy of it, like a first draft, having been found among his papers. Mickle, however, did not include it among his own works. The rival claim is made for Jean Adams, who kept a school in Greenock. The poem is included, most worthily in the " Golden Treasury of English Lyrics."

For there's nae luck about the house,
    There's nae luck ava,
There's little pleasure in the house
    When our gudeman's awa.


And are ye sure the news is true ?
    And are ye sure he's weel ?
Is this a time to think o' wark ?
    Ye jauds, fling by your wheel !
Is this a time to think o' wark,
    When Colin's at the door ?
Rax me my cloak ! I'll to the quay
    And see him come ashore.


And gie to me my bigonet,
    My bishop-satin gown,
For I maun tell the bailie's wife
    That Colin's come to town.

My Turkey slippers maun gae on,
   My hose o' pearl blue !
'Tis a' to please my ain gudeman,
   For he's baith leal and true.


Rise up and mak' a clean fireside,
   Put on the muckle pat !
Gie little Kate her cotton gown,
   And Jock his Sunday coat,
And mak' their shoon as black as slaes,
   Their hose as white as snaw !
It's a' to please my ain gudeman,
   For he's been long awa.


There's twa fat hens upon the bauk,
   Been fed this month and mair :
Mak' haste and thraw their necks about,
   That Colin weel may fare,
And mak' the table neat and clean,
   Gar ilka thing look braw !
For wha can tell how Colin fared
   When he was far awa'.


Sae true his heart, sae smooth his speech,
   His breath like caller air !
His very foot has music in't,
   As he comes up the stair.

And will I see his face again ?
    And will I hear him speak ?
I'm downright dizzy with the thought,—
    I'm troth, I'm like to greet.

For there's nae luck about the house,
    There's nae luck ava,
There's little pleasure in the house
    When our gudeman's awa.

                                        *Author unknown.*

♣          ♣          ♣

## BRAID SCOTS.

The *Scots Magazine* for November, 1743, printed this announcement (presumably by a bellringer) as " A specimen of the dialect spoke in some country places of Scotland " at that date.

All brethren and sisters, I let you to witt that there is a twa-year-auld lad littleane tint, that ist' ere'en.

It's a' scabbit i' the how hole o' the neck o'd, and a cauler kale-blade and brunt butter at it, that ist'er. It has a meickle maun blue pouch hingin at the carr side o'd, fou o' mullers and chucky-stanes, and a spindle and a whirle, and it's daddy's ain jockteleg in't. It's a' black aneath the nails wi' houkin' o' yird, that is't.
. . . It has its daddy's cravatt ty'd about the craig o'd, and hingin down the back o'd. The

55

back o' the hand o'd's a' brunt ; it got it i' t' smiddy ae day.

Wha'e'er can find this said twa-year-auld lad littleane, may repair to *M—o J—n's* town-smith in *C—n*, and he shall hae for reward quall bear sconns, and a ride o' our ain auld beast to bear him hame, and nae mair words about it, that wilt'er no.

&clubs;    &clubs;    &clubs;

## WIND WISDOM.

> When the wind's in the north,
> Hail comes forth ;
> When the wind's in the wast,
> Look for a wat blast ;
> When the wind's in the soud,
> The weather will be fresh and good ;
> When the wind's in the east,
> Cauld and snaw comes neist.
>
> *Traditional.*

&clubs;    &clubs;    &clubs;

## A SPARTAN MOTHER.

Dean Ramsay, quoting from Cockburn, appends a story that charmingly illustrates the good sense of Scottish mothers of the old school.

" There was a singular race of old Scotch ladies. They were a delightful set—strong-headed, warm-hearted, and high-spirited—merry even in solitude ; very resolute ; indifferent about the modes and habits of the modern world, and adhering to their own ways, so as to stand out like primitive rocks above ordinary society. Their prominent qualities of sense, humour, affection, and spirit, were embodied in curious outsides, for they all dressed, and spoke, and did exactly as they chose. Their language, like their habits, entirely Scotch, but without any other vulgarity than what perfect naturalness is sometimes mistaken for."

Mrs. Baird of Newbyth, the mother of our distinguished countryman the late General Sir David Baird, was always spoken of as a grand specimen of the class. When the news arrived from India of the gallant but unfortunate action of '84 against Hyder Ali, in which her son, then Captain Baird, was engaged, it was stated that he and other officers had been taken prisoner and chained together two and two. The friends were careful in breaking such sad intelligence to the mother of Captain Baird. When, however, she was made fully to understand the position of her son and his gallant companions, disdaining all weak and useless expressions of her own grief, and knowing well the restless and athletic habits of her son, all she said was,

"Lord pity the chiel that's chained to our Davy."

> Dean Ramsay : "Scottish Life and Character."

♣    ♣    ♣

## THE BUSH ABOON TRAQUAIR.

Two poems bear this title. The older version, by Robert Crawford, is far excelled in beauty by this exquisite poem by John Campbell Shairp, Principal of St. Andrew's University, first printed in his "Kilmahoe and Other Poems." Said Dr. John Brown in a letter to Shairp, "It has an unspeakable charm—the true pastoral melancholy of the region—and these long satisfying lines, like the stride of a shepherd over the crown of Minchmoor. . . I would rather have been the man to write it than Gladstone with all his greatness and goodness."

Will ye gang wi' me and fare
    To the bush aboon Traquair ?
Owre the high Minchmuir we'll up and awa',
    This bonny summer noon,
    While the sun shines fair aboon,
And the licht sklents saftly doun on holm and
    ha'.

And what would ye do there,
    At the bush aboon Traquair ?
A lang driech road, ye had better let it be ;
    Save some auld skrunts o' birk
    I' the hillside lirk,
There's nocht i' the warld for man to see.

But the blithe lilt o' that air,
"The Bush aboon Traquair,"
I need nae mair, it's eneuch for me :
Owre my cradle its sweet chime
Cam' soughin' frae auld time,
Sae tide what may, I'll awa' and see.

And what saw ye there
At the bush aboon Traquair ?
Or what did ye hear that was worth your heed ?
I heard the cushies croon
Through the gowden afternoon,
And the Quair burn singing doun to the Vale o'
Tweed.

And birks saw I three or four,
Wi' grey moss bearded owre,
The last that are left o' the birken shaw,
Whar mony a simmer e'en
Fond lovers did convene,
Thae bonny, bonny gloamin's that are lang
awa'.

Frae mony a but and ben,
By muirland, holm, and glen,
They cam' ane hour to spen' on the greenwood
sward ;
But lang hae lad an' lass
Been lying 'neth the grass,
The green, green grass o' Traquair kirkyard.

They were blest beyond compare,
When they held their trysting there
Amang thae greenest hills shone on by the sun.
And when they wan a rest,
The lownest and the best,
I' Traquair kirkyard when a' was dune.

Now the birks to dust may rot,
Names o' luvers be forgot,
Nae lads and lasses there ony mair convene ;
But the blithe lilt o' yon air
Keeps the bush aboon Traquair,
And the luve that ance was there aye fresh and
green.

*John Campbell Shairp.*

♣          ♣          ♣

## AULD COMFORTABLE DOCTRINES.

Professor Hutchinson of Glasgow University was one
of the pioneers of a more liberal theology in Scotland.
After his first sermon this verdict was given to his father by
one of the elders :—

" We a' feel muckle for your mishap ; but it
cannot be concealed. Your silly son Frank has
fashed a' the congregation with his idle cackle,
for he has been babbling this 'oor aboot a guid
and benevolent God, and that the souls o' the
heathen will gang to heaven if they follow the
licht o' their own consciences. Not a word did

the lad say, ken, or speer about the guid auld comfortable doctrines o' election, reprobation, original sin, and faith. Hoot, awa' wi' sic a fellow."

♣   ♣   ♣

## HAME.

Allan Cunningham is probably best known to English readers as the author of that stirring sea-song " A wet sheet and a flowing sea." (It is an odd fact, by the way, that some of the most popular of " English " sea-songs were written by Scots, for example : " Rule, Britannia " by James Thomson and " Ye Mariners of England " by Thomas Campbell.) But in these poignant verses Cunningham voiced the sentiments of the Scot in exile. Since he was latterly a journalist in London, we may take it that the cry was from the heart.

Hame, hame, hame, hame fain wad I be,
O, hame, hame, hame, to my ain countrie !

When the flower is i' the bud and the leaf is on
 the tree,
The larks shall sing me hame in my ain coun-
 trie.
Hame, hame, hame, hame fain wad I be,
O, hame, hame, hame, to my ain countrie !

The green leaf o' loyaltie's begun for to fa',
The bonnie white rose it is withering an' a' ;
But I'll water 't wi' the blude of usurping
 tyrannie,
An' green it will graw in my ain countrie.

O, there's naught frae ruin my country can save
But the keys o' kind heaven to open the grave :
That a' the noble martyrs wha died for loyaltie
May rise again and fight for their ain countrie.

The great are now gane, a' what ventured to
    save,
The new grass is springing on the top o' their
    grave ;
But the sun thro' the mirk blinks blythe in my
    e'e,
" I'll shine on ye yet in your ain countrie."

Hame, hame, hame, hame fain wad I be,
Hame, hame, hame, to my ain countrie !
                         *Allan Cunningham.*

        ♣       ♣       ♣

### THE TRUE PATRIARCH.

" I' my grandfather's time, as I have heard
him tell, ilka maister o' a faamily had his ain
sate in his ain hoose ; aye, an' sat wi' his hat on
his heid afore the best o' the land ; an' had
his ain dish an' wus aye helpit first an' keepit
up his authority as a man should do. Paurents
were paurents then—bairns daurdna' set up
their gabs afore them as they dae noo."
                  *Susan Ferrier : " Marriage."*

## AN EPITAPH.

This epitaph in Carluke churchyard commemorates the virtues of a departed minister :—

> A faithful holy minister here lies hid,
> One of a thousand, Mr. Peter Kid,
> Firm as a stone, but of a heart contrite,
> A wrestling, praying, weeping Israelite.

♣　　　♣　　　♣

## LIVINGSTONE'S LAST PAGE.

There is no more poignant page of manuscript in the world than the last sheet of David Livingstone's journal, written when he was stricken with a painful and mortal disease, when strength had left him and only his lion's courage remained. The tragedy of those entries in which only the date is given, is more eloquent than pages of description of the long-drawn agony could ever be.

*21st April.*—Tried to ride, but was forced to lie down, and they carried me back to vil. (*i.e.*, village) exhausted.

*22nd April.*—Carried on kitanda (a rough palaquin) over Buga S.W. $2\frac{1}{4}$.

*23rd April.*—Do.

*24th April.*—Do.

*25th April.*—Do.

*26th April.*—Do.

*27th April.*—Knocked up quite, and remain —recover—sent to buy milch goats. We are on the banks of the Molilamo. . . .

# WEE WILLIE WINKIE.

Most children of the West Country, at least, have listened to these charming domestic verses at the knee of nurse or mother. They were written in the early nineteenth century by William Miller of Parkhead, now an industrial suburb of Glasgow.

Wee Willie Winkie rins through the town,
Upstairs and doonstairs, in his nicht-gown,—
Tirlin' at the window, cryin' at the lock,
" Are the weans in their bed, for it's now ten
    o'clock ? "

Hey, Willie Winkie, are ye coming ben ?
The cat's singin' grey thrums to the sleepin'
    hen ;
The dog's spelder'd on the floor, and disna gi'e
    a cheep ;
But here's a waukrife laddie that winna fa' asleep !

Onything but sleep, you rogue ! glow'ring like
    the moon,
Rattlin' in an airn jug wi' an airn spoon,
Rumblin', tumblin', round about, crawin' like
    a cock,
Skirlin' like I kenna-what, wauk'nin sleeping folk.

Hey, Willie Winkie—the wean's in a creel !
Wamblin' aff a body's knee like a very eel,
Ruggin' at the cat's lug and ravellin' a' her
    thrums—
Hey, Willie Winkie—see, there he comes !

Wearied is the mither that has a stoorie wean—
A wee stumpie stoussie that canna rin his lane,
That has a battle aye wi' sleep before he'll close
    an e'e ;—
But ae kiss frae aff his rosy lips gi'es strength
    anew to me.

*William Miller.*

&#9827;    &#9827;    &#9827;

### THE CURLING RINK.

The great Scottish winter game brings lords and commons, farmers, ministers, and artisans on to an equality. Lord Balfour of Burleigh summed up the democracy of curling thus :—

There, if anywhere, the best man is the man who can meet the ever-changing conditions of a varying game. On one occasion when I was travelling to Carsebreck—in a third-class carriage, I might mention—I heard two friends at the other end of the carriage say, the one to the other—" Eh, Sandy, I see you are drawn ag'in a Lord." " Well, it may be so," said Sandy, " but mebbe I will be the lord before night."

&#9827;    &#9827;    &#9827;

### AN EPITAPH.

    Here lies Billy Knox,
    Wha lived and died like ither folks.

# A PHILOSOPHER'S WILL.

David Hume, the greatest of Scottish philosophers, added this codicil to his will in favour of his friend John Home, the author of *Douglas*. The two had always disputed about the merits of claret and port, the latter championed by the philosopher, and about the correct way of spelling their names, " Home " or " Hume."

I leave my friend, Mr. John Home of Kilduff, twelve dozen of my old claret at his choice, and a single bottle of that other liquor called port. I also leave him six dozen of port, provided that he attests under his hand, signed John *Hume*, that he has himself finished the bottle in two sittings. By this concession he will terminate the only two differences that ever came between us concerning temporal matters.

♣   ♣   ♣

# THE HUNDRED PIPERS.

This jolly vainglorious ballad has in it the whole military spirit of the Scots people—merry, defiant, and yet a little sad. Alas, that the jaunty tune to which it is sung cannot be reproduced here.

Wi' a hundred pipers, an' a', an' a',
Wi' a hundred pipers, an' a', an' a',
We'll up an' gi'e them a blaw, a blaw,
Wi' a hundred pipers, an' a', an' a'.
Oh, it's owre the Border, awa', awa',
It's owre the Border, awa', awa',
We'll on an' we'll march to Carlisle ha',
Wi' its yetts, its castle, an' a', an' a'.

*Wi' a hundred pipers an' a', an' a',*
*Wi' a hundred pipers an' a', an' a',*
*We'll up and gi'e them a blaw, a blaw,*
*Wi' a hundred pipers, an' a', an' a.'*

Oh ! our sodger lads look'd braw, look'd braw,
Wi' their tartan kilts, an' a', an' a',
Wi' their bonnets and feathers, an' glitt'rin' gear,
An' pibrochs sounding sweet and clear.
Will they a' return to their ain dear glen ?
Will they a' return, our Highland men ?
Second-sichted Sandy look'd fu' wae,
And mithers grat when they march'd away.

*Wi' a hundred pipers an' a', an' a',*
*Wi' a hundred pipers an' a', an' a',*
*We'll up and gi'e them a blaw, a blaw,*
*Wi' a hundred pipers an' a', an' a'.*

The Esk was swollen sae red and sae deep ;
But shouther to shouther, the brave lads keep,
Two thousand swam owre to fell English
      ground,
And danc'd themselves dry to the pibroch's
      sound.
Dumfounder'd, the English saw, they saw—
Dumfounder'd they heard the blaw, the blaw !
Dumfounder'd they a' ran awa', awa'
Frae the hundred pipers an' a', an' a'.

*Wi' a hundred pipers an' a', an' a',*
*Wi' a hundred pipers an' a', an' a',*
*We'll up an' gi'e them a blaw, a blaw,*
*Wi' a hundred pipers an' a', an' a'.*

*Lady Nairne.*

♣　　♣　　♣

## THE MEMORY OF BURNS.

This eloquent tribute to Burns was spoken by Ralph Waldo Emerson at Boston Burns Club in 1859.

The memory of Burns—I am afraid heaven and earth have taken too good care of it to leave us anything to say. The west winds are murmuring it. Open the windows behind you, and hearken for the incoming tide, what the waves say of it. The doves, perching always on the eaves of the Stone Chapel (King's Chapel), opposite, may know something about it. Every home in broad Scotland keeps his fame bright. The memory of Burns—every man's, and boy's, and girl's head carries snatches of his songs, and can say them by heart, and, what is strangest of all, never learned them from a book, but from mouth to mouth. The wind whispers them, the birds whistle them, the corn, barley, and bulrushes hoarsely rustle them ; nay, the music-boxes at Geneva are framed and toothed to play them ; the hand-organs of the Savoyards in all cities repeat them, and the chimes of bells ring them in the spires. They are the property and the solace of mankind.

        ♣       ♣      ♣

## THE PHILOSOPHICAL ANGLER.

Mr. John Buchan quotes this rhyme in his admirable anthology, *The Northern Muse*. The authorship is unknown, and we owe its preservation to Mr. Buchan, who remembers it from his youth.

*Juv.*    Canny Fisher Jamie, comin' hame at e'en,
         Canny Fisher Jamie, whaur hae ye been ?

*Pisc.*   Mony lang miles, laddie, ower the Kips
         sae green.

*Juv.*    Fishin' Leithen Water ?

*Pisc.*                Nay, laddie, nay
         Just a wee burnie rinnin' doun a brae,
         Fishin' a wee burnie nae bigger than a
         sheugh.

*Juv.*    Gat ye mony troots, Jamie ?

*Pisc.*               I gat enough—
         Eneugh to buy my baccy, snuff, and
         pickle tea,
         And lea' me tippence for a gill, and that's
         eneugh for me.

# THE SHADOW ON THE BLIND.

This passage from Lockhart's " Life of Scott " is one of the most moving and memorable in literary biography. Could anything be more dramatic than the picture of that group of hilarious young men watching, across Castle Street, the shadow of a hand that penned, night after night, the masterpieces we know as the Waverley Novels ?

It was a party of very young persons, most of them, like Menzies and myself, destined for the Bar of Scotland, all gay and thoughtless, enjoying the first flush of manhood, with little remembrance of the yesterday, or care of the morrow. When my companion's worthy father and uncle, after seeing two or three bottles go round, left the juveniles to themselves, the weather being hot, we adjourned to a library which had one large window looking northwards. After carousing here for an hour or more, I observed that a shade had come over the aspect of my friend, who happened to be placed immediately opposite to myself, and said something that intimated a fear of his being unwell. " No," said he, " I shall be well enough presently, if you will only let me sit where you are, and take my chair ; for there is a confounded hand in sight of me here, which has often bothered me before, and now it won't let me fill my glass with a good will." I rose to change places with him accordingly, and he pointed out to me this hand which, like the writing on Belshazzar's wall, disturbed his hour of hilarity. " Since we sat down," he said, " I have been watching it—it fascinates my eye— it never stops—page after page is finished and thrown on that heap of MS. and still it goes on unwearied—and so it will be till candles are brought in, and God knows how long after that. It is the same every night—I can't stand a sight of it when I am not at my books." " Some stupid, dogged, engrossing clerk, pro- bably," exclaimed myself, or some other giddy youth in our society. " No, boys," said our host, " I well know what hand it is—'tis Walter Scott's." This was the hand that, in the even- ings of three summer weeks, wrote the two last volumes of *Waverley*.

*J. G. Lockhart.*

♣　　♣　　♣

## SCOTS PROVERBS.

Corbies winna pick out corbies' een.

It's a cauld hert that canna warm its ain drink.

It's cannier to fleech a fool than to fecht him.

## "MY DEAR AND ONLY LOVE."

James Graham, Marquis of Montrose, (1612-1650) was " a bonny fechter," but he had the cavalier's love of a well-turned song. At least four lines of his poem are immortal.

My dear and only love, I pray
 That little world of thee
Be governed by no other sway
 But purest monarchy ;
For if confusion have a part,
 (Which virtuous souls abhor),
And hold a Synod in thy heart,
 I'll never love thee more.

Like Alexander I will reign.
 And I will reign alone ;
My thoughts did ever more disdain
 A rival on my throne.
He either fears his fate too much,
 Or his deserts are small,
That dares not put it to the touch
 To gain, or lose, it all.

. . . . .

But if thou wilt be faithful then,
 And constant of thy word ;
I'll make thee glorious by my pen
 And famous by my sword,

I'll serve thee in such noble ways
    Were never heard before !
I'll crown and deck thee with all bays,
    And love thee evermore.
          *James Graham, Marquis of Montrose.*

♣      ♣      ♣

## THE CALL OF THE BAGPIPE.

Englishmen have pretended to believe that the fondness of the Scot for the music of the pipes is a patriotic pretence. This passage from " John Splendid " helps to explain the reality of the emotion.

On a sudden there rose away before us towards the mouth of the glen the sound of a bagpipe. It came on the tranquil air with no break in its uproar, and after a preparatory tuning it broke into an air called " Cogadh no Sith "—an ancient braggart pibroch made by one Macruimen of the Isle of Skye—a tune that was commonly used by the Campbells as a night-retreat or tattoo.

My heart filled with the strain. It gave me not only the simple illusion that I saw again the regimentals of my native country—many a friend and comrade among them in the shelter of the Castle of Inverlochy—but it roused in me a spirit very antique, very religious and moving too, as the music of his own land must in every honest Gael.

" *Cruachan* for ever ! " I said lightly to M'Iver, though my heart was full.

He was as much touched by that homely lilt as myself. " The old days, the old styles ! " said he. " God ! how that pibroch stings me to the core ! " And as the tune came more clearly in the second part, or *Crunluadh* as we call it, and the player maybe came round a bend of the road, my comrade stopped in his pace and added with what in another I might have thought a sob—" I've trudged the world ; I have learned many bravadoes, so that my heart never stirred much to the mere trick of an instrument but one, and the *piob mhor* conquers me. What is it, Colin, that's in us, rich and poor, yon rude cane-reeds speak so human and friendly to ? "

" 'Tis the Gaelic," I said, cheered myself by the air. " Never a roar of the drone or a sob of the chanter but's in the Gaelic tongue."

" Maybe," said he, " maybe : I've heard the scholars like yourself say the sheepskin and the drones were Roman—that or Spanish, it's all one to me. I heard them at Boitzenburg when we gave the butt of the gun to Tilly's *soldadoes*, they played us into Holstein, and when the

ditch of Stralsund was choked with the tartan
of Mackay, and our lads were falling like corn
before the hook, a Reay piper stood valiantly in
front and played a salute.  Then and now it's
the pipes, my darling ! "

*Neil Munro : " John Splendid."*

♣ ♣ ♣

## CHALLENGE TO THE WORLD.

The following words were first uttered in Scots by George
Keith, fifth Earl Marischal (1553–1623) who founded
Marischal College in Aberdeen.  His family had been
enriched by Church lands and the phrase was Keith's
retort to those who questioned his right of possession.
George Bernard Shaw had them carved on his mantelpiece :—

They say.                  They saye.
What say they ?            Quhat saye thay ?
Let them say !             Let thaim saye !

♣ ♣ ♣

## BONNIE PRINCE CHARLIE.

This story has been pieced together from various diaries
and contemporary records—the " Journal " of David, Lord
Elcho, " The Lyon in Mourning," by Robert Forbes, etc.
The saga opens with a serving-man's account of the landing
in the Hebrides.

Two or three hours before landing, an eagle
came hovering over the frigate, and continued
so to do till they were all safe on shore. . . .
The Duke of Athol . . . turning to the Prince

said, " Sir I hope this is an excellent omen, and promises good things to us. The king of birds is come to welcome your royal highness upon your arrival in Scotland." . . . When they landed in Eriska, they could not find a grain of meal or one inch of bread. But they catched some flounders, which they roasted upon the bare coals in a mean low hut they had gone into near the shore, and Duncan Cameron stood cook. The Prince sat at the cheek of the little ingle, upon a fail sunk, and laughed heartily at Duncan's cookery.

Arrived in Edinburgh, the Prince lived in glorious state, a King among his own people. The account is by Lord Elcho.

The Prince lived in Ednr from the 22 of Sept to the 31 of Octr, with Great Splendour and Magnificence, had Every morning a numerous Court of his Officers. After he had held a Councill, he dinn'd with his principall officers in publick, where their was always a Crowd of all sorts of people to See him dine. After dinner he rode out Attended by his life guards and review'd his Army, where their was always a great number of Spectators in Coaches and on horseback. After the review he Came to the Abbey, where he received the ladies of fashion that came to his drawing-room. Then he

Sup'd in publick, and Generaly their was musick at Supper, and a Ball afterwards.

Then followed the foolish invasion of England, which ended at Derby. The Prince had to turn back and finally faced Cumberland at Culloden. Again Lord Elcho is responsible for this account of the battle.

It was a dark, misty, rainy day, & the wind blew in the face of the Princes army. Their was no manner of Councill held upon the Field. . . . On Wednesday the 16 of April 1746, about half an hour after Eleven, the Duke of Cumberlands army appeared two miles off, Straight in front of the Princes. . . . The Dukes army Continued always advancing and keeping a Continued fire both of Canon and muskettery, which killed a vast number of the Princes people. At last when they were very near, the word of Command to Advance was given, and all the line moved forward, but in the advancing the whole left wing of the Princes army gave way, and run away without firing their musketts ; the Centre join'd the right and in a Sort of mob, without any order or distinction of Corps, mixt together, rush'd in and attack'd the Dukes left wing, and broke the regiments opposite to them in the first line, but the Second line marching up beat them off, and obliged them to turn their backs, and run away. . . . The

Prince who at the beginning of the Action was behind the Irish piquetts guarded by Sixteen of Fitzjames's horse, turn'd about his horse and went off as soon as the left wing gave way, and never offer'd to rally any of the broken Corps; but indeed it would have been to no purpose, for none of the highlanders who Escaped ever Stop'd untill they gott home to their own houses.

It was on this occasion that Elcho sped the Prince from the battlefield with the bitter jibe:

" There you go for a damned cowardly Italian."

Then followed the flight, in the course of which the Prince passed to Skye disguised as a " Bettie Burk " in the company of Flora MacDonald. This was the passport he used:

" I have sent your daughter from this country lest she should be in any way frightened with the troops lying here. She has got one Bettie Burk, an Irish girl, who as she tells me is a good spinster. If her spinning pleases you, you may keep her till she spin all your lint; or if you have any wool to spin you may employ her,—I am, your dutyful husband,

Hugh MacDonald."

Even in exile and something like disgrace, the Prince retained his attractiveness for women.

After Miss Flora had got up, Mrs. Mac-Donald told her that she wanted much to have a lock of the Prince's hair, and that she behoved to go into his room and get it for her. Miss Flora refused to do as she desired, because the Prince was not yet out of bed. " What then," said Mrs. MacDonald, " no harm will happen to you. He is too good to harm you or any person. You must instantly go in and get me the lock." Mrs. MacDonald, opening the door, said, " Sir, it is I, and I am importuneing Miss Flora to come in and get a lock of your hair to me, and she refuses to do it." " Pray," said the Prince, " desire Miss MacDonald to come in. What should make her afraid to come where I am ? " When Miss came in he begged her to sit down on a chair at the bedside, then laying his arms about her waist, and his head upon her lap, he desired her to cut out the lock with her own hands in token of future and more substantial favours. The one half of the lock Miss gave to Mrs. MacDonald and the other she kept to herself.

And Donald Macleod, a serving-man, examined by the Hanoverian General Campbell, could proudly declare his loyalty to his defeated Prince.

The General asked if he had been along with the young Pretender ? " Yes," said Donald, " I was along with that young gentleman, and I winna deny it." " Do you know," said the General, " what money was upon that man's

79

head ? No less a sum than *thirty thousand pounds sterling*, which would have made you and all your children after you happy for ever."
. . . "What then ? *thirty thousand pounds !* Though I had gotten 't I could not have enjoyed it eight and forty hours. Conscience would have gotten up upon me. That money could not have kept it down. And tho' I could have gotten all England and Scotland for my pains I would not allowed a hair of his body to be touched if I could help it."

But the adventure ended ignominiously, and in this passage from the narrative of MacDonald of Kingsburgh we hear " the end of an auld sang."

I heard Mrs. MacDonald of Kingsburgh say that she had the following particulars from Malcolm MacLeod's own mouth. . . . Malcolm went with the Prince and MacKinnon to the shore to see them fairly boated for the Continent. When he was about to take leave of the Prince he spied some ships coming in sight and hovering about the coast. He intreated the Prince not to go on board for some time, but to wait till he should see how these ships steer'd their course ; " For just now," said he, " the wind blows so as to fetch them this way and to hinder your passing to the Continent." The Prince replied, " Never fear, MacLeod,

I'll go on board directly. The wind will change immediately and make these ships steer a contrary course. Providence will take care of me, and it will not be in the power of these ships to look near me at this time. . . ." The Prince and his retinue had not rowed many yards from the shore till the wind changed to a point directly opposite to what it had been.

☘ ☘ ☘

## A FAT SHEEP TO KILL.

Fresh meat was so little known in eighteenth century Scotland that in burgh towns in Forfarshire " there was often no butcher, and when a man in the district had a calf or few sheep for sale, the bellman went round advertising the people to come and buy."—(*Farmer's Magazine*, 1806). The only butcher in Lanark was a weaver by trade, who before killing a sheep took good care that the minister, provost, and bailies took shares. The fact was announced by the bellman :—

Bell-ell-ell,
There's a fat sheep to kill,
A leg for the provost,
Another for the priest ;
The bailies and the deacons
They'll tak' the rest ;
And if the fourth leg we cannot sell,
The sheep it maun live and gang back to the hill.
*Chambers : " Popular Rhymes."*

## SIR WALTER.

The Scotch national character originates in many circumstances ; first of all, in the Saxon stuff there was to work on ; but next, and beyond all else except that, in the Presbyterian Gospel of John Knox. It seems a good national character ; and, on some sides, not so good. Let Scott thank John Knox, for he owed him much, little as he dreamed of debt in that quarter ! No Scotchman of his time was more entirely Scotch than Walter Scott : the good and the not so good, which all Scotchmen inherit, ran through every fibre of him.

*Thomas Carlyle.*

&#9827;　　&#9827;　　&#9827;

## HOMESICKNESS.

Happy the craw
　That biggs in the Trotten shaw,
And drinks o' the Water o' Dye—
　For nae mair may I.

*Author unknown.*

&#9827;　　&#9827;　　&#9827;

## A CATHEDRAL SAVED.

That Glasgow Cathedral alone among all the Scottish cathedrals, survived the destructive furies of the Reformation is still a fair joke against the commercial instincts of the Second City. No account of how the edifice was saved is racier than that spoken by Andrew Fairservice in "Rob Roy."

"Ah! it's a brave kirk—nane o' yere whig-maleeries and curliewurlies and opensteek hems about it—a' solid, well-jointed mason-wark, that will stand as lang as the warld, keep hands and gun-powther aff it. It had amaist a douncome lang syne at the Reformation, when they pu'd down the kirks of St. Andrews and Perth, and thereawa', to cleanse them o' Papery, and idolatry, and image-worship, and surplices, and sic lik rags o' the muckle hure that sitteth on seven hills, as if ane wasna braid eneugh for her hinder end. Sae the commons o' Renfrew, and o' the Barony, and the Gorbals, and a' about, they behoved to come into Glasgow ae fair morning, to try their hand on purging the High Kirk o' Popish nick-nackets. But the townsmen o' Glasgow, they were feared their auld edifice might slip the girths in gaun through siccan rough physic, sae they rang the common bell, and assembled the train-bands wi' took o' drum. By good luck the worthy James Rabat was Dean o' Guild that year (and a gude mason he was himsell, made him the keener to keep up the auld biggin) ; and the trades assembled, and offered downright battle to the commons, rather than their kirk should coup the crans, as others

had done elsewhere. It wasna for love o'
Paperie—na, na !—nane could ever say that o'
the trades o' Glasgow—sae they sune came to an
agreement to take a' the idolatrous statues of
sants (sorrow be on them) out o' their neuks.
And sae the bits o' stane idols were broken in
pieces by Scripture warrant, and flung into the
Molendiner burn, and the auld kirk stood as
crouse as a cat when the flaes are kaimed aff her,
and a'body was alike pleased. And I hae heard
wise folk say, that if the same had been done in
ilka kirk in Scotland, the Reform wad just hae
been as pure as it is e'en now, and we wad hae
mair Christian-like kirks ; for I hae been sae
lang in England, that naething will drived out
o' my head, that the dog-kennel at Osbaldistone
Hall is better than mony a house o' God in
Scotland.

*Sir Walter Scott : " Rob Roy."*

♣          ♣          ♣

**A POTENT DRINK.**

The authorship of this stanza is unknown. The careful
observer will note that it was adapted by Burns in " My
luve's she's but a lassie yet."

We're a' dry wi' the drinkin' o't,
  We're a' dry wi' the drinkin' o't,
The minister kissed the fiddler's wife,
And he couldna preach for thinkin' o't.

## SCOTCH BROTH.

Even Dr. Johnson paid a grudging tribute to the excellences of the national dish.

At dinner, Dr. Johnson ate several plate-fulls of Scotch broth, with barley and peas in it, and seemed very fond of the dish. I said, " You never ate it before." Johnson. " No, sir ; but I don't care how soon I eat it again."

> *James Boswell : " Journal of a Tour to the Hebrides."*

♣    ♣    ♣

## AN EPITAPH.

This inscription is on the tombstone in Reid Kirkyard, Annandale, of one John Bell, who flourished in the seventeenth century.

I Jocky Bell o' Braikenbrow, lyes under this
    stane,
    Five of my awn sons laid it on my wame ;
I liv'd aw my dayes, but sturt or strife,
    Was man o' my meat, and master o' my
    wife.
If you done better in your time, than I did in
    mine,
    Take the stane aff my wame, and lay it on o'
    thine.

## BUILDERS OF EMPIRE.

George Douglas Brown was a shrewd, if hardly sympathetic, judge of the national character, and "The House with the Green Shutters" is rich in illuminating passages, such as this on the ambitious quality of the Scot.

That the Scot is largely endowed with the commercial imagination his foes will be ready to acknowledge. Imagination may consecrate the world to a man, or it may merely be a visualising faculty which sees that, as already perfect, which is still lying in the raw material. The Scot has the lower faculty in full degree ; he has the forecasting leap of the mind which sees what to make of things—more, sees them made and in vivid operation. To him there is a railway through the desert where no railway exists, and mills along the quiet stream. And his *perfervidum ingenium* is quick to attempt the realising of his dreams. That is why he makes the best of colonists. Galt is his type—Galt, dreaming in boyhood of the fine water power a fellow could bring round the hill from the stream where he went a-fishing (they have done it since), dreaming in manhood of the cities yet to rise amid Ontario's woods (they are there to witness to his foresight). Indeed, so flushed and riotous can the Scottish mind become over a commercial prospect that it sometimes sends native caution by the board, and a man's really fine idea becomes an empty balloon, to carry him off to the limbo of vanities. There is a megalomaniac in every parish of Scotland. Well, not so much as that; they're owre-canny for that to be said of them. But in every district, almost, you may find a poor creature who for thirty years has cherished a great scheme by which means to revolutionise the world's commerce, and amass a fortune in monstrous degree. He is generally to be seen shivering at the Cross, and (if you are a nippy man) you shout carelessly in going by, "Good-morning, Tamson; how's the scheme?" And he would be very willing to tell you, if only you would wait to listen. "Man," he will cry eagerly behind you, "if I only had anither wee wheel in my invention—she would do, the besom! I'll sune have her ready noo." Poor Tamson!

*George Douglas Brown : " The House with the Green Shutters."*

♣     ♣     ♣

**PROVERB.**

They say in Fife
That next to nae wife
The best thing is a guid wife.

## THE CANDID FATHER.

James Boswell's father, Lord Auchinleck, made this pithy comment on his son's attachment to Dr. Johnson :—

" Jamie has gaen clean gyte. What do you think, man ? He's dune wi' Paoli—he's aff wi' the land-loupin' scoondrel o' a Corsican. Whae's tail do ye think he has preened himsel' tae noo ? A dominie man !—an auld dominie, wha keepit a schule and caa'ed it an Acaademy ! "

♣ ♣ ♣

## A NURSERY RHYME.

This rhyme does not read like the work of him who penned the " Ode to a Nightingale " but Keats was capable of high spirits in his letters. This nonsense was sent to his sister from Kirkcudbright.

There was a naughty boy
And a naughty boy was he.
He ran away to Scotland,
The people for to see.
 But he found
 That the ground
 Was as hard,
 That a yard
 Was as long
 That a song
 Was as merry,
 That a cherry

Was as red,
That lead
Was as weighty,
That four-score
Was still eighty,
  And a door was as wooden as in England.
So he stood in his shoes and he wondered,
He wondered, he wondered,
So he stood in his shoes and he wondered.

*John Keats.*

♣     ♣     ♣

## THE TERRIBLE GLEN.

Glencoe has always impressed the traveller. Dorothy Wordsworth's description of its grandeur is well known, but perhaps more effective is this passage from a letter by Dickens quoted in Forster's " Life."

All the way, the road had been among moors and mountains with huge masses of rock, which fell down God knows where, sprinkling the ground in every direction, and giving it the aspect of the burial place of a race of giants. Now and then we passed a hut or two, with neither window nor chimney, and the smoke of the peat fire rolling out at the door. But there were not six of these dwellings in a dozen miles ; and anything so bleak and wild, and mighty in its loneliness, as the whole country, it is impossible to conceive. Glencoe itself is perfectly *terrible*. The pass is an awful place. It is shut in on each side by enormous rocks from which great torrents come rushing down in all directions. In amongst these rocks on one side of the pass (the left as we came) there are scores of glens, high up, which form such haunts as you might imagine yourself wandering in, in the very height and madness of a fever. They will live in my dreams for years—I was going to say as long as I live, and I seriously think so. The very recollection of them makes me shudder. . . .

*Charles Dickens.*

♣    ♣    ♣

## THE TWENTY-THIRD PSCHALME.

This, the best-loved of the Psalms, was thus beautifully paraphased by Alexander Montgomerie, who was in the service of Regent Morton and James VI., and in his devout old age published all the Psalms in metrical form.

The Lord maist hie
I know will be
An herd to me ;
I cannot lang have stress, nor stand in neid ;
He makes my lair
In fields maist fair,
Quhair I bot care,
Reposing at my pleasure, safety feid.

He sweetly me convoys,
Quhair naething me annoys,
But pleasure brings.
He brings my mynd
Fit to sic kynd,
That foes, or fears of foe cannot me grieve.
He does me leid
In perfect freid,
And for his name he never will me lieve.
Thoch I wald stray,
Ilk day by day,
In deidly way,
Yet will I not dispair ; I fear none ill,
For quhy thy grace
In every place,
Does me embrace,
Thy rod and shepherd's crook me comfort still.
In spite of foes
My tabil grows,
Thou balms my head with joy ;
My cup owerflows.
Kyndness and grace,
Mercy and peice,
Sall follow me for all my wretched days,
And me convoy,
To endless joy,
In heaven quhair I sall be with thee always.
                                    *Alexander Montgomerie.*

# THE ORIGINAL OF ROBINSON CRUSOE.

The following extract from the fascinating *Statistical Account* of Scotland, compiled from information mainly supplied by parish ministers in the nineties of the eighteenth century, provides an interesting sidelight on an English masterpiece.

Alexander Selkirk, who was rendered famous by Mons. de Foe, under the name of Robinson Crusoe, was born in Largo, 1676. His history, divested of fable, is as follows :—

Having gone to sea in his youth, and in the year 1703, being sailing master of the ship "Cinque Ports," Captain Stradling, bound for the South Seas, he was put on shore on the island of Juan Fernandez, as a punishment for mutiny. In that solitude he remained for four years and four months, from which he was at last relieved and brought to England by Captain Woods Rogers. He had with him in the island his clothes and bedding, with a firelock, some powder, bullets and tobacco, a hatchet, knife, kettle, his mathematical instruments, and Bible. He built two huts of Pimento trees, and covered them with long grass, and in a short time lined them with skins of goats which he killed with his musket, so long as his powder lasted (which at first was but a pound) ; when that was spent he caught them by speed of foot. Having learned to produce fire by rubbing two pieces of wood together, he dressed his victuals in one of his huts and slept in the other, which was at some distance from his kitchen. A multitude of rats often disturbed his repose by gnawing his feet and other parts of his body, which induced him to feed a number of cats for his protection. In a short time these became so tame that they would lie about him in hundreds, and soon delivered him from the rats, his enemies. Upon his return, he declared to his friends that nothing gave him so much uneasiness as the thoughts, that when he died his body would be devoured by those very cats he had with so much care tamed and fed. To divert his mind from such melancholy thoughts, he would sometimes dance and sing among his kids and goats, at other times retire to his devotion. His clothes and shoes were soon worn, by running through the woods. In the want of shoes he found little inconvenience, as the soles of his feet became so hard that he could run everywhere without difficulty. As for his clothes, he made for himself a coat and a cap of goats' skins, sewed with little thongs of the same cut into proper form with his knife. His only needle was a nail. When his knife was worn to the back, he made others as well as he could of some iron hoops that had been left on shore, by beating them thin and grinding them on stones. By his long seclusion from intercourse with men, he had so far forgot the use of speech, that the people on board Captain Rogers's ship could scarce understand him for he seemed to speak his words by halves. The chest and musket which Selkirk had with him on the island are now (1790) in the possession of his grand-nephew John Selkirk, weaver in Largo.

♣    ♣    ♣

## JONAH AND THE WHALE.

Zachary Boyd was a Scots divine of the seventeenth century who, possessing more piety than poetry, turned a dozen of the greatest stories in Scripture into 26,080 lines of incredibly bad verse. The result was quaint, as these extracts from his account of Jonah's adventure prove :—

*The Sailors.* Now over boord hee throwne is
    by and by,
Where in the waters he doth sprawling ly :
There Jonah is, God's wrath for to appease,
Ev'n head and eares downe soused in the seas.

    But what is this that near him wee doe see,
Like to a tower wambling on the sea ;
A monster great, the Leviathan strong,
With beame like jawes that followes him along :
A little space the whale did round him play,
To waite his time, but in a short delay

94

He wheel'd about, and in a trice wee sawe
The living man he buri'd in his mawe.

Jonah is later made to lament his fate as follows :—

I understood that God was good and kind,
But mongrell thoughts with foly pierc'd my
    mind,
Heere apprehended, I in prison ly,
What goods will ransome my captivity ?
What house is this, where's neither fire nor
    candle,
Where I no thing but guts of fishes handle ?
*Zachary Boyd.*

Zachary Boyd was too good a target to be missed by the
wits and the enemies of Presbyterianism, one of whom,
Samuel Colvill, in his " The Whig's Supplication," fastened
on poor Boyd parodies that are even better remembered than
their models. Thus Colvill made Boyd deliberately put on
record :—

There was a man called Job
    Dwelt in the land of Uz,
He had a good gift of the gob ;
    The same case happen us !

Another part of Job's story was declared to be :—

Job's wife said to Job,
    Curse God and die.
O no, you wicked scold,
    No, not I.

And into Boyd's mouth was put this version :—

> And Jacob made for his wee Josie,
> A tartan coat to keep him cosie ;
> And what for no ? there was nae harm
> To keep the lad baith saft and warm.
>
> *Samuel Colvill.*

♣    ♣    ♣

## THE POWER OF POETRY.

Which is the more beautiful, Loch Lomond or Loch Katrine, is a question hardly worth debating, but this amusing note from Shairp's edition of Dorothy Wordsworth's " Recollections of a Tour " shows that the comparison was once a matter of acute professional jealousy.

When Mr. Jamieson, the editor of the fifth edition of Burt's Letters, was in the Highlands in 1814, four years after the publication of Scott's Poem, and eleven after the Wordsworths' visit, he met a savage-looking fellow on the top of Ben Lomond, the image of " Red Murdoch," who told him that he had been a guide to the mountain for more than forty years, but now " a Walter Scott " had spoiled his trade. " I wish," said he, " I had him in a ferry over Loch Lomond ; I should be after sinking the boat, if I drowned myself into the bargain, for ever since he wrote his ' Lady of the Lake,' as they call it, everybody goes to see that filthy hole, Loch Ketterine. The devil confound his ladies and his lakes ! "

## IN EXILE.

Another characteristically Scottish expression of nostalgia. In *The Northern Muse*, Mr. John Buchan acknowledges his indebtedness for the lines to Mrs. Violet Jacob.

Oh, gin I were a doo,
I wad flee awa' the noo
Wi' my neb to the Lomonds an' my wings
    wavin' steady,
An' I wadna rest a fit,
Till at gloamin' I wad sit
Wi' ither neebor doos on the lums o' Balgeddie.

&#9827;   &#9827;   &#9827;

## THE END OF A QUEEN.

This remarkable account of the execution of Mary Queen of Scots, was written by an eye-witness of the proceedings, Samuel Tomascon, who communicated it to the great mercantile house, the Fuggers of Augsburg, whose agent he was.

The Earl of Kent said to her : " Madame, I am grieved on your account to hear of this superstition from you and to see that which is in your hand." She said it was seemly that she should hold the figure of Christ in her hand thereby to think of Him. Thereupon he answered that she must have Christ in her heart, and further said that though she made demur in paying heed to the mercies vouchsafed to her by God All-Highest, they would nevertheless plead for her with God Almighty, that He would forgive her sins and receive her into His Kingdom. Thereto the Queen made reply : " Pray, then will I also pray." Then the aforesaid Doctor fell on his knees on the steps of the dais and read in an over-loud voice a fervent and godly prayer for her, most suitable to such an occasion, also for the Queen of England and the welfare of the Kingdom. All those standing round repeated the prayer. But as long as it lasted the Queen was praying in Latin and fairly audibly, holding the crucifix in her hand.

When the prayer was now ended on both sides, the executioner knelt in front of the Queen. Him she forgave his deed, as also all those who lusted after her blood, or desired her death. She further forgave all and sundry and craved from God that He might also forgive her own trespasses. Thereafter she fell on her knees in ardent supplication and besought the remission of her sins. She said that she trusted to be saved through the death of Christ and His Blood and that she was ready to have her own blood spilt at His feet, wherefore she held His picture and the crucifix in her hands. Further she prayed for a happy, long and prosperous reign for the Queen of England, for the prosperity of the British Isles, for the afflicted Christian Church and the end of all misery.

She also prayed for her son, the King of Scots, for his upright and honourable Government and of his conversion to the Catholic Faith. At the last she prayed that all the saints in heaven might intercede for her on this day, and that God of His great goodness might avert great plagues from this Island, forgive her her sins and receive her soul into His heavenly hand.

Thereupon she stood up and prepared herself for death. She doffed her jewels and her gown, with the help of two women. When the executioner wished to assist her, she said to him that it was not her wont to be disrobed in the presence of such a crowd, nor with the help of such handmaidens. She herself took off her robe and pushed it down as far as the waist. The bodice of the underskirt was cut low and tied together at the back. She hastened to undo this.

Thereafter she kissed her ladies, commending them to God, and because one of them was weeping too loudly, she said to her : " Have I not told you that you should not weep ? Be comforted." To her she gave her hand, and bade her leave the dais. When she was thus prepared, she turned to her servitors, who were kneeling not far off, blessed them and made them to pray for her. Afterwards she fell on her knees with great courage, did not change colour, and likewise gave no sign of fear. As she knelt down she repeated the 70th Psalm : " *In te, Domine, speravi. . . .*" When she had said this to the end, she, full of courage, bent down with her body and laid her head on the block, exclaiming : " In manus tuas, Domine, commendo spiritum meum." Then one of the executioners held down her hands, and the other cut off her head with two strokes of the chopper. Thus ended her life.

The executioner took the head and showed it to the people, who cried : " God spare our Queen of England ! "

When the executioner held up the head, it fell in disarray so that it could be seen that her hair was quite grey and had been closely cropped.

Her raiment and other belongings were by command taken from the executioner, but he was promised their equivalent in money. Everything that had been sprinkled with her blood, also the garments of the executioner and other objects, were promptly taken away and washed. The planks of the dais, the black cloth and all else were thrown into the fire, at once, so that no superstitious practices could be carried on therewith.

Her body was carried out, embalmed and made ready for burial. Where this will take place is as yet unknown. Her servants and courtiers were instructed to abide there until her remains had been honourably laid to rest. She was four-and-forty years of age, and was the most beautiful princess of her time.

*From " The Fugger News Letters."*

♣ ♣ ♣

**A WEATHER RHYME.**

If Candlemas Day be fair and clear
The half o' winter's to gang an' mair.
If Candlemas Day be dark and foul.
The half o' Winter's past at Yule.

*Traditional.*

♣ ♣ ♣

**UNDER THE CRUST.**

" . . . I hope you liked your jaunt, Miss Bell ? "

" It wasn't bad," said Bell, putting out the cards. " But, mercy on me ! what a silly way they have of baking bread in England—all crust outside, though I grant it's sweet enough when you break into it."

" H'm ! " said Dr. Brash. " I've seen Scotch folk a bit like that."

*Neil Munro : " The Daft Days."*

# IT WAS A' FOR OUR RIGHTFU' KING.

One of the finest of Jacobite songs, believed to have been written by Captain Ogilvie of Inverquharity, who fought at the Battle of the Boyne and followed the Old Pretender into exile in France.

" It was a' for our rightfu' King
We left fair Scotland's strand,
It was a' for our rightfu' King
We e'er saw Irish land, my dear,
We e'er saw Irish land.

Now a' is done that men can do,
And a' is done in vain :
My love an' native land, fareweel,
For I maun cross the main, my dear,
For I maun cross the main."

He turned him right an' round about,
Upon the Irish shore,
An' ga'e his bridle-rein a shake,
With, " Adieu for evermore, my dear,"
With, " Adieu for evermore."

" *The Sodger frae the wars returns,*
*The sailor frae the main :*
*But I hae parted frae my love,*
*Never to meet again, my dear,*
*Never to meet again.*

*When day is gane, an' night is come,*
*An' a' folk bound to sleep,*
*I think on him that's far awa',*
*The lee-lang night, an' weep, my dear,*
*The lee-lang night, an' weep."*
      *Ogilvie of Inverquharity.*

  &clubs;   &clubs;   &clubs;

## DR. JOHNSON—JACOBITE.

I here began to indulge old Scottish sentiments, and to express a warm regret, that, by
our Union with England, we were no more ;—
our independent kingdom was lost.—JOHNSON :
" Sir, never talk of your independency, who
could let your Queen remain twenty years in
captivity, and then be put to death, without even
a pretence of justice, without your ever attempt-
ing to rescue her ; and such a Queen too ! as
every man of any gallantry of spirit would have
sacrificed his life for."

   *James Boswell : " Journal of a Tour to*
    *the Hebrides."*

  &clubs;   &clubs;   &clubs;

## AN EPITAPH.

   Here lie I, Martin Elginbrodde :
   Hae mercy o' my soul, Lord God ;
   As I wad do, were I Lord God,
   And ye were Martin Elginbrodde.

## OATMEAL.

Johnson's *Dictionary* : " Oats, a grain which in England is generally given to horses, but in Scotland supports the people."

Lord Elibank : " But where will you find such men and such horses ? "

    ☘     ☘     ☘

## FLODDEN FIELD.

But as they left the darkening heath,
More desperate grew the strife of death.
The English shafts in volleys hailed,
In headlong charge their horse assailed :
Front, flank, and rear, the squadrons sweep
To break the Scottish circle deep,
    That fought around their king.
But yet, though thick the shafts as snow,
Though charging knights like whirlwinds go,
Though bill-men ply the ghastly blow,
    Unbroken was the ring ;
The stubborn spearmen still made good
Their dark impenetrable wood,
Each stepping where his comrade stood,
    The instant that he fell.
No thought was there of dastard flight ;
Linked in the serried phalanx tight,
Groom fought like noble, squire like knight,
    As fearlessly and well ;

Till utter darkness closed her wing.
O'er their thin host and wounded king.
Then skilful Surrey's sage commands
Led back from strife his shattered bands ;
     And from the charge they drew,
As mountain-waves from wasted lands
     Sweep back to ocean blue.
Then did their loss his foemen know ;
Their king, their lords, their mightiest low,
They melted from the field as snow,
When streams are swoln and south winds blow,
     Dissolves in silent dew.
Tweed's echoes heard the ceaseless plash,
While many a broken band,
Disordered, through her currents dash,
     To gain the Scottish land ;
To town and tower, to down and dale,
To tell red Flodden's dismal tale,
And raise the universal wail.
Tradition, legend, tune, and song
Shall many an age that wail prolong :
Still from the sire the son shall hear
Of the stern strife and carnage drear
     Of Flodden's fatal field,
Where shivered was fair Scotland's spear,
     And broken was her shield !
             *Scott : " Marmion."*

## MICHAELMAS EVE.

Old rhyme with which Nairn children collected their fairings on Michaelmas Eve :—

To-night's the market evening,—
To-morrow's the market day,—
And we shall get our fairings,
And we shall march away.
    The cock shall crow,
    The hen shall lay,
    The drum shall beat,
    And the pipe shall play,
For to-morrow is the merry, merry market-day.
                 *Traditional.*

♣      ♣      ♣

## ARCHIEPISCOPAL ANGER.

This, surely the most comprehensive curse ever devised, was issued in the early years of the sixteenth century by Gavin Dunbar, Archbishop of Glasgow, to be read by parish priests against any who contravened the laws of the Church.

I curse their head and all the hairs of their head, I curse their face, their eyes, their mouth, their nose, their tongue, their teeth, their shoulders, their back, and their heart, their arms, their legs, their hands, their feet, and every part of their body, from the top of their head to the sole of their feet. Before and behind, within and without. I curse them walking and I curse them riding. I curse them standing and I curse them sitting. I curse them eating and I curse them drinking, I curse them waking and I curse them sleeping. I curse them within the house and I curse them without the house. I curse their wives, their bairns and their servants. I curse their cattle, their wool, their sheep, their horse, their swine, their geese, and their hens. I curse their halls, their chambers, their stables and their barns. The malediction of God that lit upon Lucifer, that struck him from the high Heaven to the deep Hell shall light upon them. The fire and the sword that stopped Adam from the gates of Paradise shall stop them from the gloir of Heaven until they forbear and make amends. I dissever, and part them from the Kirk of God, and deliver them quick to the devill of Hell, as the Apostle Paul delivered Corinthion. And finally, I condemn them perpetually to the deep pit of Hell, to remain with Lucifer and all his fellows. And as these candles go from your sight, so may their souls go from the visage of God, and their good frame from the world, until they forbear their open sins and rise from this terrible cursing and make satisfaction and penance.

# THE TWA CORBIES.

This grim ballad is believed to record the treacherous murder of a nobleman by his faithless wife. Set to a haunting minor melody, it is to be found in several collections of songs.

As I was walking all alane,
I heard twa corbies making a mane,
The tane unto the t'other say,
" Where sall we gang and dine to-day ? "

" In behint yon auld fail dyke,
I wot there lies a new-slain knight ;
And nae body kens that he lies there,
But his hawk, his hound, and lady fair.

" His hound is to the hunting gane,
His hawk to fetch the wild-fowl hame,
His lady's ta'en another mate,
So we may mak' our dinner sweet.

" Ye'll sit on his white hause-bane,
And I'll pike out his bonny blue een :
Wi' ae lock o' his gowden hair
We'll theek our nest when it grows bare.

" Mony a ane for him makes mane,
But nane sall ken whare he is gane :
O'er his white banes, when they are bare,
The wind sall blaw for evermair."

*Traditional.*

# DEMOCRATIC EDUCATION.

The Parish School was the ancient pride of Scotland—before the Education Acts—but every community of any size offered various facilities for polite education. There is no more amusing description of these irregular institutions than that penned by Sir James M. Barrie in "Sentimental Tommy."

There were at this time three schools in Thrums, the chief of them ruled over by the terrible Cathro (called Knuckly when you were a street away from him). It was a famous school, from which a band of three or four or even six marched every autumn to the universities as determined after bursaries as ever were Highlandmen to lift cattle, and for the same reason, that they could not do without.

A very different kind of dominie was Cursing Ballingall, who had been dropped at Thrums by a travelling circus, and first became familiar to the town as, carrying two carpet shoes, two books, a pillow and a saucepan, which were all his belongings, he wandered from manse to manse offering to write sermons for the ministers at circus prices. That scheme failing, he was next seen looking in at windows in search of a canny calling, and eventually he cut one of his braces into a pair of tawse, thus with a single stroke of the knife, making himself a schoolmaster and lop-sided for life. His fee was but a penny a week, " with a bit o' the swine when your father kills," and sometimes there were so many pupils on a form that they could only rise as one. During the first half of the scholastic day Ballingall's shouts and pounces were for parents to listen to, but after his dinner of crowdy, which is raw meal and hot water, served in a cogie, or wooden bowl, languor overcame him and he would sleep, having first given out a sum in arithmetic and announced :

" The one as finds out the answer first, I'll give him his licks."

Last comes the Hanky School, which was for the genteel and for the common who contemplated soaring. You were not admitted to it in corduroys or barefooted, nor did you pay weekly ; no, your father called four times a year with the money in an envelope. He was shown into the blue-and-white room, and there, after business had been transacted, very nervously on Miss Ailie's part, she offered him his choice between ginger wine and what she falteringly called wh-wh-whisky. He partook in the polite national manner, which is thus :

" You will take something, Mr. Cortachy ? "

" No, I thank you, ma'am."

" A little ginger wine ? "

" It agrees ill with me."

" Then a little wh-wh-whisky ? "
" You are ower kind."
" Then may I ? "
" I am not heeding."
" Perhaps, though, you don't take ? "
" I can take it or want it."
" Is that enough ? "
" It will do perfectly."
" Shall I fill it up ? "
" As you please, ma'am."

*J. M. Barrie : " Sentimental Tommy."*

♣　　♣　　♣

## WITCHCRAFT.

Isobel Goudie, burned as a witch in 1662, declared in a confession that this was the charm she used when desirous of changing herself into a hare :—

I sall go intill a hare,
With sorrow, sigh, and muckle care ;
And I sall go in the devil's name,
Ay while I come back again.

The corresponding charm for turning herself into her natural shape ran thus :—

Hare, hare, God send thee care ;
I am in a hare's likeness now,
But I sall be a woman e'en now ;
Hare, hare, God send thee care.

*Pitcairn : " Criminal Trials in Scotland."*

## MEG DODS ON DEATH.

" Ay, and is it even sae ? " said Meg ; " and
has the puir bairn been sae soon removed frae
this fashious warld ?  Ay, ay, we maun a' gang
ae gate—crackit quart stoups and geisened
barrels—leaky quaighs are we a', and canna
keep in the water o' life—Ohon, sirs ! "
*Sir Walter Scott : " St. Ronan's Well."*

♣     ♣     ♣

## FINE FLOWERS IN THE VALLEY.

This is a peculiarly compact and characteristic specimen
of the ballad.  An origin in historical fact is suggested by
the alternative title, " Lady Anne."

She sat down below a thorn,
   *Fine flowers in the valley ;*
And there she has her sweet babe born,
   *And the green leaves they grow rarely.*

" Smile na sae sweet, my bonny babe,
   *Fine flowers in the valley,*
An ye smile sae sweet, ye'll smile me dead,"
   *And the green leaves they grow rarely.*

She's ta'en out her little penknife,
   *Fine flowers in the valley,*
And twine'd the sweet babe o' its life,
   *And the green leaves they grow rarely.*

She's howket a grave by the light o' the moon,
*Fine flowers in the valley,*
And there she's buried her sweet babe in,
*And the green leaves they grow rarely.*

As she was going to the church,
*Fine flowers in the valley,*
She saw a sweet babe in the porch,
*And the green leaves they grow rarely.*

" O sweet babe, an thou were mine,
*Fine flowers in the valley,*
I wad clead thee in silk so fine,"
*And the green leaves they grow rarely.*

" O mother dear, when I was thine,
*Fine flowers in the valley,*
Ye did na prove to me sae kind,"
*And the green leaves they grow rarely.*

*Traditional.*

☙　　☙　　☙

## THE SKY RAINS BLOOD.

Upone the 28 of Maii 1650, thair rayned bluid, be the space of thrie myles, in the Erle of Bukcleuchis boundis, upone the landis of — neir to the Englische bordouris ; quhilk wes verifeyit in presence of the Committee of Stait.

*John Nicoll : " Diary."*

## KILMENY.

The comparison between this quotation from Hogg's lovely poem and "Tam o' Shanter" (see p. 123) is peculiarly interesting. Burns could deal with the grotesque, but Hogg could suggest magic—a gift unusual among Scottish poets. It has been suggested that Sir James Barrie found the central idea of his play, "Mary Rose," in these beautiful lines.

Bonnie Kilmeny gaed up the glen ;
But it wasna to meet Duneira's men,
Nor the rosy monk of the isle to see,
For Kilmeny was pure as pure could be.
It was only to hear the yorlin sing,
And pu' the cress-flower round the spring ;
The scarlet hypp and the hind-berrye,
And the nut that hangs frae the hazel tree ;
For Kilmeny was pure as pure could be.
But lang may her minny look o'er the wa' ;
And lang may she seek i' the green-wood shaw ;
Lang the laird o' Duneira blame,
And lang, lang greet or Kilmeny come hame !

When many a day had come and fled,
When grief grew calm, and hope was dead,
When mess for Kilmeny's soul had been sung,
When the bedesman had pray'd and the dead-
    bell rung,
Late, late in a gloamin' when all was still,
When the fringe was red on the westlin hill,

The wood was sere, the moon i' the wane,
The reek o' the cot hung over the plain,
Like a little wee cloud in the world its lane ;
When the ingle lowed wi' an eiry leme—
Late, late in the gloaming Kilmeny came hame !

" Kilmeny, Kilmeny, where have you been :
Lang hae we sought baith holt and dean ;
By linn, by ford, and green-wood tree,
Yet you are halesome and fair to see.
Where gat ye that joup o' the lily sheen ?
That bonnie snood o' the birk sae green ?
And these roses, the fairest that ever were seen ?
Kilmeny, Kilmeny, where have you been ? "

Kilmeny, look'd up wi' a lovely grace,
But nae smile was seen on Kilmeny's face ;
As still was her look, and as still was her e'e,
As the stillness that lay on the emerant lea,
Or the mist that sleeps on a waveless sea.
For Kilmeny had been, she knew not where,
And Kilmeny had seen what she could not
    declare ;
Kilmeny had been where the cock never crew,
Where the rain never fell, and the wind never
    blew.
But it seemed as the harp of the sky had rung,
And the airs of heaven played round her tongue,

When she spake of the lovely forms she had
    seen,
And a land where sin had never been ;
A land of love and a land of light,
Withouten sun, or moon, or night ;
Where the river swa'd a living stream,
And the light a pure celestial beam ;
The land of vision, it would seem,
A still, an everlasting dream.

*James Hogg.*

♣      ♣      ♣

## THE SMELLS OF EDINBURGH.

The housewives of old Edinburgh were notoriously careless in their handling of household refuse. " Gardy loo ! "
they cried in the old French phrase, and emptied their
buckets into the street from high windows.  This famous
passage from Boswell contains Dr. Johnson's comment on
hygiene in the capital.

I heard a late baronet of some distinction in
the political world in the beginning of the
present reign, observe, that " walking in the
streets of Edinburgh at night was pretty perilous,
and a good deal odiferous."  The peril is much
abated, by the care which the magistrates have
taken to enforce the city laws against throwing
foul water from the windows ; but, from the
structure of the houses in the old town, which
consist of many stories, in each of which a

different family lives, and there being no covered sewers, the odour still continues. A zealous Scotsman would have wished Mr. Johnson to be without one of his five senses upon this occasion. As we marched slowly along, he grumbled in my ear, " I smell you in the dark ! "

> *James Boswell : " Journal of a Tour to the Hebrides."*

♣   ♣   ♣

## AE FOND KISS.

Whatever the depth of Burn's passion for " Clarinda " (Mrs. Maclehose), the affair produced this immortal love-song.

Ae fond kiss, and then we sever !
Ae fareweel, alas, for ever !
Deep in heart-wrung tears I'll pledge thee,
Warring sighs and groans I'll wage thee.
Who shall say that fortune grieves him
While the star of hope she leaves him ?
Me, nae cheerfu' twinkle lights me,
Dark despair around benights me.

I'll ne'er blame my partial fancy,
Naething could resist my Nancy ;
But to see her was to love her,
Love but her, and love for ever.

Had we never lov'd sae kindly,
Had we never lov'd sae blindly,
Never met—or never parted,
We had ne'er been broken-hearted.

Fare thee weel, thou first and fairest !
Fare thee weel, thou best and dearest !
Thine be ilka joy and treasure,
Peace, enjoyment, love, and pleasure.
Ae fond kiss, and then we sever ;
Ae fareweel, alas, for ever !
Deep in heart-wrung tears I'll pledge thee,
Warring sighs and groans I'll wage thee.

*Robert Burns.*

♣       ♣       ♣

## THE RUINS OF IONA.

This " purple patch," renowned in literary history,
embodies Dr. Johnson's most generous tribute to a
Scottish scene.

We were now treading that illustrious Island,
which was once the luminary of the Caledonian
regions, whence savage clans and roving bar-
barians derived the benefits of knowledge, and
the blessings of religion. To abstract the mind
from all local emotions would be impossible, if
it were endeavoured, and would be foolish if
it were possible. Whatever withdraws us from
the power of our senses, whatever makes the
past, the distant, or the future, predominate

over the present, advances us in the dignity of thinking beings. Far from me, and from my friends, be such frigid philosophy as may conduct us indifferent and unmoved over any ground which has been dignified by wisdom, bravery, or virtue. That man is little to be envied, whose patriotism would not gain force upon the plain of *Marathon*, or whose piety would not grow warmer among the ruins of *Iona !*

*Samuel Johnson : " Journey to the Hebrides."*

\* \* \*

## WILL YE NO COME BACK AGAIN ?

This Jacobite song, set to a fine broad melody, is now in effect the national song of parting on sorrowful occasions.

Bonnie Charlie's noo awa,
 Safely o'er the friendly main ;
Mony a heart will break in twa,
 Should he ne'er come back again.

  *Will ye no come back again ?*
  *Will ye no come back again ?*
  *Better lo'ed ye canna be.*
  *Will ye no come back again ?*

Ye trusted in your Hieland men,
 They trusted you, dear Charlie !
They kent your hiding in the glen,
 Death and exile braving.

English bribes were a' in vain,
    Tho' puir and puirer we maun be ;
Siller canna buy the heart
    That aye beats warm for thine and thee.

We watched thee in the gloamin' hour,
    We watched thee in the mornin' grey ;
Though thirty thousand pounds they gie,
    Oh, there is nane that wad betray !

Sweet's the laverock's note, and lang,
    Liltin' wildly up the glen ;
But aye to me he sings ae sang,
    " Will ye no come back again ? "

> *Will ye no come back again ?*
> *Will ye no come back again ?*
> *Better lo'ed ye canna be.*
> *Will ye no come back again ?*
>                 *Baroness Nairne.*

&#9827; &#9827; &#9827;

## HOW JOHN KNOX PREACHED.

The following is a contemporary account of Knox's manner and ardour in preaching at St. Andrews, in 1571, the year before his death.

In the opening up of his text he was moderat, the space of ane half houre, but when he enterit to application, he made me so to grew and tremble, that I could not hold a pen to wryte. He was very weik. I saw him everie

day of his doctrine go hulie and fear ; with a
furring of marticks about his neck, a staff in
the ane hand, and gud godlie Richart Ballanden,
his servant, holding up the uther oxter, from
the abbey to the parish kirk ; and he, the said
Richart, and another servant, lifted up to the
pulpit, where he behovit to lean, at his first
entrie ; bot er he haid done with his sermone,
he was sa active and vigorous that he was lyk to
ding the pulpit in blads, and flie out of it.

*Melville : " Life of Knox."*

♣ ♣ ♣

## MARY MORISON.

" One of my juvenile works—not very remarkable either
for its merits or demerits," said Burns of this, one of the
loveliest love-songs ever written !

O Mary, at thy window be,
  It is the wish'd, the trysted hour !
Those smiles and glances let me see,
  That make the miser's treasure poor :
How blythely wad I bide the stoure,
  A weary slave frae sun to sun,
Could I the rich reward secure,
  The lovely Mary Morison.

Yestreen, when to the trembling string
  The dance gaed thro' the lighted ha',
To thee my fancy took its wing,
  I sat, but neither heard nor saw :

Tho' this was fair, and that was braw,
    And yon the toast of a' the town,
I sigh'd, and said amang them a',
    " Ye are na Mary Morison."

O Mary, canst thou wreck his peace,
    Wha for thy sake wad gladly die ?
Or canst thou break that heart of his,
    Whase only faut is loving thee ?
If love for love thou wilt na gie,
    At least be pity to me shown !
A thought ungentle canna be
    The thought o' Mary Morison.
                                *Robert Burns.*

❧        ❧        ❧

SCOTS PROVERBS.

It's ill getting the breeks aff a Hielandman.

Keep your ain fish-guts to your ain sea-maws.

Kindness creeps where it canna gang.

Better a finger aff than aye waggin'.

He that will to Cupar maun to Cupar.

It's nae mair pity to see a woman greet nor to see a goose go barefit.

# TAM O' SHANTER'S ORDEAL.

When the Scot treats of the uncanny, it is generally in witches, rather than in fairies, that he is interested. It is instructive to compare this passage from " Tam o' Shanter " with the passage from Hogg's " Kilmeny " printed on page 114.

The wind blew as 'twad blawn its last ;
The rattling show'rs rose on the blast ;
The speedy gleams the darkness swallow'd ;
Loud, deep, and lang, the thunder bellow'd :
That night, a child might understand,
The Deil had business on his hand.
Weel mounted on his gray mare, Meg,
A better never lifted leg,
Tam skelpit on thro' dub and mire,
Despising wind, and rain, and fire ;
Whiles holding fast his gude blue bonnet ;
Whiles crooning o'er some auld Scots sonnet ;
Whiles glow'ring round wi' prudent cares,
Lest bogles catch him unawares.
Kirk-Alloway was drawing nigh,
Whare ghaists and houlets nightly cry.
By this time he was cross the ford,
Where in the snaw the chapman smoor'd ;
And past the birks and meikle stane,
Where drunken Charlie brak's neck-bane ;
And thro' the whins, and by the cairn,
Where hunters fand the murder'd bairn ;

And near the thorn, aboon the well,
Where Mungo's mither hang'd hersel.
Before him Doon pours all his floods ;
The doubling storm roars thro' the woods ;
The lightnings flash from pole to pole ;
Near and more near the thunders roll :
When, glimmering thro' the groaning trees,
Kirk-Alloway seem'd in a bleeze ;
Thro' ilka bore the beams were glancing ;
And loud resounded mirth and dancing. . . .

And, vow !  Tam saw an unco sight !
Warlocks and witches in a dance !
Nae cotillon brent new frae France,
But hornpipes, jigs, strathspeys, and reels,
Put life and mettle in their heels.
A winnock-bunker in the east,
There sat auld Nick, in shape o' beast—
A touzie tyke, black, grim, and large !
To gie them music was his charge :
He screw'd the pipes and gart them skirl,
Till roof and rafters a' did dirl.
Coffins stood round like open presses,
That shaw'd the dead in their last dresses ;
And by some devilish cantraip sleight
Each in its cauld hand held a light,
By which heroic Tam was able
To note upon the haly table

A murderer's banes in gibbet-airns ;
Twa span-lang, wee, unchristen'd bairns ;
A thief new-cutted frae the rape—
Wi' his last gasp his gab did gape ;
Five tomahawks, wi' blude red rusted ;
Five scymitars, wi' murder crusted ;
A garter, which a babe had strangled ;
A knife, a father's throat had mangled,
Whom his ain son o' life bereft—
The gray hairs yet stack to the heft ;
Wi' mair of horrible and awfu',
Which even to name wad be unlawfu'.

*Robert Burns.*

♣    ♣    ♣

## THE RIDING OF THE PARLIAMENT.

The assemblies of the old Scots Parliament, or Estates, were preceded by a solemn procession on horseback from Holyrood to the Parliament House near St. Giles. An eminent Scottish historian gives us here a picture that must cause the patriot to deplore the loss of colour in the national life.

The procession, according to old feudal usage, began diminutively, and swelled in importance as it went. The representatives of the burghs went first ; then, after a pause, came the lesser barons, or county members ; and then the nobles—the highest in rank going last. A herald called each name from a window of the palace, and another at the gate saw that the member took his place in the train. All rode two abreast. The commoners wore the heavy doublet of the day unadorned. The nobility followed in their gorgeous robes. Each burghal commissioner had a lackey, and each baron two, the number increasing with the rank, until a duke had eight. The nobles were each followed by a trainbearer, and the Commissioner was attended by a swarm of decorative officers, so that the servile elements in the procession must have dragged it out to a considerable length. It seems, indeed, to have been borrowed from the French processions, and was full of glitter—the lackeys, over their liveries, wearing velvet coats embroidered with armorial bearings.

All the members were covered, save those whose special function it was to attend upon the honours—the crown, sceptre, and sword of state. These were the palladium of the nation's imperial independence, and the pomp of the procession was concentrated on the spot where they were borne—the same as they may yet be seen in Edinburgh Castle—before the Commissioner. Immediately before the sword rode the Lord Lyon, in his robe and heraldic overcoat, with his chain and baton. Behind him were clustered a clump of gaudy heralds and pursuivants, with noisy trumpeters proclaiming the approach of the precious objects which they guarded. Such was the procession which poured into that noble oak-roofed hall, which still recalls, by its name and character, associations with the ancient legislature of Scotland.

*Hill Burton : " History of Scotland."*

## NO POPERY.

"The Gude and Godlie Ballatis" were a collection of satirical and religious poems of the Reformation time, said to be the work of three brothers named Wedderburn, of Dundee. This is probably the most famous of these poems ; it was founded on a secular song, whose words survive oddly in the chorus :

The Paip, that pagane full of pryde,
  He hes us blindit lang ;
For quhair the blind the blind dois gyde,
  Na wonder thay ga wrang :
Lyke prince and king he led the ring
  Of all iniquitie :
Hay trix, tryme go trix,
  Under the grene-wod tree.

Bot his abominatioun
  The Lord hes brocht to licht ;
His Popifche pryde, and thrinfalde crowne,
  Almaift hes loist thair micht ;
His plak pardounis ar bot lardounis
  Of new found vanitie :
Hay trix, tryme go trix, &c.

We went to the Cottage and took some whisky. I wrote a sonnet for the mere sake of writing some lines under the roof : they are so bad I cannot transcribe them. The man at the cottage was a great bore with his anecdotes. I hate the rascal. His life consists in fuzy, fuzzy, fuzziest. He drinks glasses, five for the quarter, and twelve for the hour ; he is a mahogany-faced old jackass who knew Burns : he ought to have been kicked for having spoken to him. He calls himself " a curious old bitch," but he is a flat old dog. I should like to employ Caliph Vathek to kick him. Oh, the flummery of a birth-place ! Cant ! cant ! cant ! It is enough to give a spirit the guts-ache. Many a true word, they say, is spoken in jest—this may be because his gab hindered my sublimity ; the flat dog made me write a flat sonnet. My dear Reynolds, I cannot write about scenery and visitings. Fancy is indeed less than present palpable reality, but it is greater than remembrance. You would lift your eyes from Homer only to see close before you the real Isle of Tenedos. You would rather read Homer afterwards than remember yourself. One song of Burns's is of more worth to you than all I could think for a whole year in his native country. His misery is a dead weight upon the nimbleness of one's quill; I tried to forget it—to drink toddy without any care—to write a merry sonnet—it won't do —he talked, he drank with blackguards; he was miserable. We can see horribly clear, in the works of such a man, his whole life, as if we were God's spies.

*John Keats : " Letters."*

Keats's sonnet on this occasion is more interesting as a curiosity than impressive as a poem :—

This mortal body of a thousand days
Now fills, O Burns, a space in thine own room,
Where thou didst dream alone on budded bays,
Happy and thoughtless of thy day of doom !
My pulse is warm with thine old Barley-bree,
My head is light with pledging a great soul,
My eyes are wandering, and I cannot see,
Fancy is dead and drunken at its goal ;
Yet can I stamp my foot upon thy floor,
Yet can I ope thy window-sash to find
The meadow thou hast tramped o'er and
    o'er,—
Yet can I think of thee till thought is blind,—
Yet can I gulp a bumper to thy name,—
O smile among the shades, for this is fame !

*John Keats.*

## AY WAUKIN', O.

This is one of Burns's most beautiful " reconstructions " of pre-existing material. Mr. Buchan points out that the first verse and chorus are old. The last verse, moreover, is also to be found in the Ulster folk song, " I know where I'm going."

O I'm wat, wat,
    O I'm wat and wearie !
Yet fain wad I rise and rin,
    If I thought I would meet my dearie.

Ay waukin', O !
    Waukin' ay, and wearie,
Sleep I can get nane
    For thinkin' on my dearie.

Simmer's a pleasant time,
    Flowers of every colour,
The water rins ower the heugh—
    And I lang for my true lover.

When I sleep I dream,
    When I wauk I'm eerie ;
Sleep I can get nane
    For thinkin' on my dearie.

Lanely night comes on ;
    A' the lave are sleepin' ;
I think on my love,
    And bleer my een wi' greetin'.

Feather-beds are saft,
  Pentit rooms are bonnie ;
But a kiss o' my dear love
  Is better far than ony.

*Robert Burns.*

Dr. John Brown's commentary on the poem is delightful :

" A ploughman or shepherd—for I hold that it is a man's song—comes in ' wat, wat ' after a hard day's work among the furrows or on the hill. The *watness* of wat, wat, is as much wetter than wet as a Scotch mist is more of a mist than an English one ; and he is not only wat, wat, but ' weary,' longing for a dry skin and a warm bed and rest ; but no sooner said and felt than, by the law of contrast, he thinks on ' Mysie ' or ' Ailie,' his Genevieve ; and then ' all thoughts, all passions, all delights ' begin to stir him, and ' fain wad I rise and rin ' (what a swiftness beyond ' run ' is ' rin ' !). Love now makes him a poet, the true imaginative power enters and takes possession of him. By this time his clothes are off, and he is snug in bed ; not a wink can he sleep ; that ' fain ' is domineering over him—and he breaks out into what is as genuine passion and poetry as anything from Sappho to Tennyson—abrupt, vivid, heedless of syntax. ' Simmer's a pleasant time.' Would any of our greatest geniuses, being limited to one word, have done better than take ' pleasant ' ? and then the fine vagueness of ' time ' ! ' Flowers of every colour '; he gets a glimpse of ' herself a fairer flower,' and is off in pursuit. ' The water rins over the heugh ' (a steep precipice); flinging itself wildly, passionately over, and so do I long for my true lover. Nothing can be simpler and finer than

> When I sleep I dream ;
> When I wauk I'm eerie.'

' Lanely nicht ': how much richer and more touching than ' darksome.' ' Feather beds are saft '; ' pentit rooms are bonnie '; I would infer from this, that this ' dearie,' his ' true love,' was a lass up at ' the big house '—a dapper Abigail possible—at Sir William's at the Castle."

*Dr. John Brown : " Horæ Subsecivæ."*

⁂

## AN EPITAPH.

This laconic inscription—challenged on the score of brevity only by the curt " Poor White " in a graveyard on Lochfyneside—was copied from a stone in the wall of the church at Dowallie, Perthshire.

> Here lys
> James Stewart
> He sall rys.

## THE LAND O' THE LEAL.

I'm wearin' awa', John,
Like snaw-wreaths in thaw, John ;
I'm wearin' awa'
    To the land o' the leal.
There's nae sorrow there, John,
There's neither cauld nor care, John :
The day is aye fair
    In the land o' the leal.

Our bonnie bairn's there, John,
She was baith gude and fair, John ;
And oh ! we grudged her sair
    To the land o' the leal.
But sorrow's sel' wears past, John,
And joy's a-comin' fast, John—
The joy that's aye to last
    In the land o' the leal.

Sae dear's that joy was bought, John,
Sae free the battle fought, John,
That sinfu' man e'er brought
    To the land o' the leal.
Oh, dry your glist'ning e'e, John !
My saul langs to be free, John ;
And angels beckon me
    To the land o' the leal.

Oh, haud ye leal and true, John !
Your day it's wearin' thro', John ;
And I'll welcome you
    To the land o' the leal.
Now fare ye weel, my ain John,
This warld's cares are vain, John ;
We'll meet, and we'll be fain
    In the land o' the leal.

*Lady Nairne.*

&#9827;　　&#9827;　　&#9827;

## ORIGIN OF A SUPERSTITION.

That poor silly Jeezabel, our Queen Mary,
married that lang-legged ne'er do-weel, Darnley,
in the month of May, and ever sin syne the
Scots folks have regarded it as no canny.

*Reginald Dalton.*

&#9827;　　&#9827;　　&#9827;

## THE WEARY GHOST'S LAMENT.

Wae's me, wae's me,
The acorn's not yet
Fallen from the tree
That's to grow the wood,
That's to make the cradle,
That's to rock the bairn,
That's to grow a man,
That's to lay me.

*Traditional.*

## THE FAITH OF A COVENANTER.

This beautiful letter was written to her husband by one, Janet Lintoun, imprisoned in Dunottar Castle in 1685 on account of her Covenanting principles.

My dear heart, bless the Lord on my behalf, that ever it should hav pleased such a holy God to have looked upon such an unworthy sinner as I am, or to hav honoured the like of me to suffer anay thing for his name's saik, or bear his cross in a day when ther is so few longing to wear his livery. . . . The Lord has made all things easy to me and he has been soe kind to my soul somtyms since I came to prison, that I counted all things nothing in comparison of him. . . . *Now*, my dear, ye are dear, indeed, to me, bot not soe dear as Christ. . . . My love, I ken not what the Lord will doe with me ; bot I think I will see you although I should be banished out of my nativ land. Although enemies have separat our bodies, they shall never separat my love from you. . . .

♣      ♣      ♣

## POACHING IN EXCELSIS.

(" Two men were fined £120 apiece for poaching a white rhinoceros."—*South African Press*.)

I've poached a pickle paitricks when the leaves
    were turnin' sere,
I've poached a twa-three hares an' grouse, an'
    mebbe whiles a deer,

But ou, it seems an unco thing, an' jist a wee
  mysterious,
Hoo any mortal could contrive tae poach a
  rhinocerious.

I've crackit wi' the keeper, pockets packed wi'
  pheasants' eggs,
An' a ten-pun' saumon hangin' doun in baith
  my trouser legs,
But eh, I doot effects wud be a wee thing
  deleterious
Gin ye shuld stow intil yer breeks a brace o'
  rhinocerious.

I mind hoo me an' Wullie shot a Royal in
  Braemar,
An' brocht him doun tae Athol by the licht o'
  mune an' star.
An' eh, Sirs ! but the canny beast contrived tae
  fash an' weary us—
Yet staigs maun be but bairn's play beside a
  rhinocerious.

I thocht I kent o' poachin' jist as muckle's ither
  men,
But there is still a twa-three things I doot I
  dinna ken ;

An' noo I cannot rest, my brain is growin' that
    deleerious
Tae win awa' tae Africa an' poach a rhino-
    cerious.

G. K. Menzies.

      &clubs;      &clubs;      &clubs;

## SCOTTISH TOASTS.

May the winds of adversity ne'er blow open our
    door.
May the hinges of friendship ne'er rust, or the
    wings of love lose a feather.
May the mouse ne'er leave our meal pock with
    the tear in its eye.
When we are going up the hill of fortune may
    we ne'er meet a friend coming down.

      &clubs;      &clubs;      &clubs;

## AN EPITAPH.

This epitaph in dialogue and verse is to be found in
varying forms in several parts of the country. Scots
humour has a distinct leaning towards the *macabre*.

" Wha lies here ?
Wha lies here ? "
" Wee Tammy Twenty, ye needna spier."
" Eh ! Tammy, is that you ? "
" Atweel is't—but I'm deed noo ! "

Traditional.

## TRUE WISDOM.

I knew a very wise man who believed that if a man were permitted to make all the ballads, he need not care who should make the laws of the nation.

*Fletcher of Saltoun.*

&clubs;     &clubs;     &clubs;

## PROUD MAISIE.

Scott puts this haunting song into the mouth of the dying Madge Wildfire in " The Heart of Midlothian."

Proud Maisie is in the wood,
   Walking so early ;
Sweet Robin sits on the bush,
   Singing so rarely :

" Tell me, thou bonny bird,
When shall I marry me ? "
" When six braw gentlemen
Kirkward shall carry ye."

" Who makes the bridal bed,
Birdie, say truly ? "
" The grey-headed sexton
That delves the grave duly.

" The glow-worm o'er grave and stone
   Shall light thee steady ;
The owl from the steeple sing :
   ' Welcome, proud lady.' "

*Sir Walter Scott.*

## BYRON ON SCOTT.

I see the *Lady of the Lake* advertised. Of course it is in his old ballad style and pretty. After all, Scott is the best of them. The end of all scribblement is to amuse, and he certainly succeeds there. I long to read his new romance. . . . He is undoubtedly the Monarch of Parnassus, and the most *English* of bards.

*Byron, in a Letter.*

♣     ♣     ♣

## A LYKE-WAKE DIRGE.

This wonderful dirge may have been born just South of the Border, but only a balladist in the closest touch with Scottish sentiment and the Scottish tongue could have produced it.

This ae nighte, this ae nighte,
   *Every nighte and alle,*
Fire, and sleet, and candle-lighte ;
   *And Christe receive thye saule.*

When thou from hence away art paste,
   *Every nighte and alle,*
To Whinny-muir thou comest at laste ;
   *And Christe receive thye saule.*

If ever thou gavest hosen and shoon,
   *Every nighte and alle,*
Sit thee down and put them on ;
   *And Christe receive thye saule.*

If hosen and shoon thou ne'er gavest nane,
   *Every nighte and alle,*
The whinnes sall pricke thee to the bare bane ;
   *And Christe receive thye saule.*

From Whinny-muir when thou mayst passe,
   *Every nighte and alle,*
To Brig o' Dread thou comest at laste ;
   *And Christe receive thye saule.*

From Brig o' Dread when thou mayst passe
   *Every nighte and alle,*
To purgatory fire thou comest at laste ;
   *And Christe receive thye saule.*

If ever thou gavest meate or drinke,
   *Every nighte and alle,*
The fire sall never make thee shrinke :
   *And Christe receive thye saule.*

If meate or drinke thou gavest nane,
   *Every nighte and alle,*
The fire will burn thee to the bare bane ;
   *And Christe receive thye saule.*

This ae nighte, this ae nighte,
   *Every nighte and alle,*
Fire, and sleet, and candle-lighte ;
   *And Christe receive thye saule.*
                                        *Traditional.*

# THE SCOTCH KIRK.

Buckle, one of the severest critics of post-Reformation Scotland, permitted himself this scathing, but not wholly unjustified, passage on Scotland in the seventeenth century :—

On this account, it was improper to care for beauty of any kind ; or, to speak more accurately, there was no real beauty. The world afforded nothing worth looking at, save and except the Scotch Kirk, which was incomparably the most beautiful thing under heaven. To look at that was a lawful enjoyment, but every other pleasure was sinful. To write poetry, for instance, was a grievous offence, and worthy of especial condemnation. To listen to music was equally wrong ; for men had no right to disport themselves in such idle recreation. Hence the clergy forbad music to be introduced even during the festivities of a marriage ; neither would they permit, on any occasion, the national entertainment of pipers. Indeed, it was sinful to look at any exhibition in the streets, even though you only looked at it from your own window. Dancing was so extremely sinful, that an edict, expressly prohibiting it, was enacted by the General Assembly and read in every church in Edinburgh. New Year's Eve had long been a period of rejoicing in Scotland, as in other parts of Europe. The

Church laid her hands on this also, and ordered that no one should sing the songs usual on that day, or should admit such singers into his own private house.

H. T. Buckle, " *The History of Civilization in England.*"

❧　　❧　　❧

## ANNIE LAURIE.

Probably Scotland's most popular love song, and set to an air as widely and affectionately known as that of " Auld Lang Syne."

Maxwellton braes are bonnie,
　Where early fa's the dew,
And it's there that Annie Laurie
　Gie'd me her promise true ;
Gie'd me her promise true ;
　That ne'er forgot sall be ;
But for bonnie Annie Laurie
　I'd lay doun my head and dee.

Her brow is like the snaw-drift,
　Her neck is like the swan,
Her face it is the fairest
　That e'er the sun shone on ;
That e'er the sun shone on,
　And dark blue is her e'e ;
And for bonnie Annie Laurie
　I'd lay doun my head and dee.

Like dew on the gowan lying
    Is the fa' o' her fairy feet ;
And like winds in simmer sighing,
    Her voice is low and sweet ;
Her voice is low and sweet,
    And she's a' the world to me,
And for bonnie Annie Laurie
    I'd lay doun my head and dee.

*Lady John Scott.*

Annie Laurie actually lived, the daughter of Laurie of
Maxwellton in Dumfriesshire.   An older version of the song,
written about 1680, was the work of one Douglas of Fingland,
whose devotion, however, did not win the lady's hand, for
she married the Laird of Craigdarroch.   His second verse,
printed below, compares very unfavourably with that in
Lady John Scott's much later version.

She's backit like the peacock,
    She's breastit like the swan ;
She's jimp about the middle,
    Her waist ye well micht span.
Her waist ye well micht span,
    And she has a rolling eye ;
And for bonnie Annie Laurie
    I'd lay me down and die.

*Douglas of Fingland.*

♣      ♣      ♣

**THE POWER OF BRAID SCOTS.**

The phrases " Celtic glamour," and " Celtic
twilight," have become somewhat vague and

hackneyed, and Lowland Scotch is not especially Celtic in origin or character. And yet we certainly have derived from Scotland a remarkable vocabulary, expressive of gloom and mystery ; and in words like *murk*, *gloaming*, *glamour*, *gruesome*, *fey*, *freit*, *bogle*, *warlock*, *wraith*, *eerie*, *eldritch*, *uncanny*, and *second sight*, we find good examples of expressive power in local dialects, and learn how a standard language may enrich itself by drawing on their resources.

*Logan Pearsall Smith in " Words and Idioms."*

&clubs;     &clubs;     &clubs;

NURSERY RHYMES.

Little girls playing at ball used to recite these ancient verses :—

> Stottie ba', hinnie ba', tell to me
> How many bairns am I to hae ?
> Ane to leeve and ane to dee
> And ane to sit on the nurse's knee !

Spoken by children while holding some object concealed in one hand from their companions who were expected to guess rightly or lose the gift :—

> Nievie, nievie, nick-nack,
> Which hand will ye tak ?
> Tak the richt, tak the wrang,
> I'll beguile ye if I can.

*Traditional.*

## GREAT SAYINGS OUT OF SCOTS HISTORY.

" I have brought you to the ring and now you must dance."—Sir William Wallace to his men at the battle of Falkirk.

" If God gives me but a dog's life, I will make the key to keep the castle and the bracken bush the cow."—James I of Scotland.

" It cam' with a lass and it will gang with a lass."—James V on hearing of the birth of his daughter Mary, later Queen of Scots.

" There's ane end of ane auld sang."—Lord Chancellor Seafield at the Union of the Parliaments.

♣   ♣

## DROWNED IN YARROW.

The shortest and most poignant of many versions of a moving ballad.

Willy's rare, and Willy's fair,
    And Willy's wondrous bonny ;
And Willy hecht to marry me
    Gin e'er he married ony.

Yestreen I made my bed fu' braid,
    This night I'll make it narrow ;
For a' the live-lang winter night
    I lie twin'd of my marrow.

O came you by yon water-side,
    Pou'd you the rose or lily ?
Or came you by yon meadow green ?
    Or saw you my sweet Willy ?
She sought him east, she sought him west,
    She sought him braid and narrow ;
Syne in the cleaving of a craig
    She found him drown'd in Yarrow.

*Traditional.*

☙    ☙    ☙

**WHAT KNOX DID.**

We must spare a few words for Knox ;
himself a brave and remarkable man ; but still
more important as Chief Priest and Founder,
which one may consider him to be, of the Faith
that became Scotland's, New England's, Oliver
Cromwell's. . . . This that Knox did for his
Nation, I say, we may really call a resurrection
as from death. It was not a smooth business ;
but it was welcome surely, and cheap at that
price, had it been far rougher. On the whole
cheap at any price—as life is. The people began
to *live :* they needed first of all to do that, at what
cost and costs soever. Scotch Literature and
Thought, Scotch Industry ; James Watt, David
Hume, Walter Scott, Robert Burns : I find
Knox and the Reformation acting in the heart's

core of every one of these persons and pheno-
mena ; I find that without the Reformation
they would not have been.

> *Carlyle : " Heroes and Hero-Worship."*

&clubs;     &clubs;     &clubs;

## FAIRY RINGS.

The fate of the farmer who was so impious as to plough
up a fairy ring or otherwise disturb the haunts of the little
people is here contrasted with the good fortune of the man
who treated them with respect.

> He wha tills the fairies' green
>   Nae luck again shall hae.
> And he wha spills the fairies' ring
>   Betide him want and wae ;
> For weirdless days and weary nichts
>   Are his till his deein' day.
>
> He wha gaes by the fairy ring
>   Nae dule nor pine shall see ;
> And he wha cleans the fairy ring
>   An easy death shall dee.

> *Traditional.*

&clubs;     &clubs;     &clubs;

## AN ANCIENT SATIRE.

When heather-bells grow cockle-shells
The miller and the priest will forget them-
sel's.

> *Traditional.*

## TO THE CUCKOO.

This charming poem has been the subject of one of the
sharpest controversies in Scottish literary history. Generally
it is ascribed to John Logan, who was at one time a minister,
but the claim of Michael Bruce, who was a college friend
of Logan's, has also been asserted vigorously. Logan's
views of literary propriety were not too exalted, but during
his lifetime his authorship of the poem was never disputed.

Hail, beauteous stranger of the grove !
    Thou messenger of Spring !
Now Heaven repairs thy rural seat,
    And woods thy welcome ring.

What time the daisy decks the green,
    Thy certain voice we hear ;
Hast thou a star to guide thy path,
    Or mark the rolling year ?

Delightful visitant ; with thee
    I hail the time of flowers,
And hear the sound of music sweet
    From birds among the bowers.

The school-boy, wand'ring through the wood
    To pull the primrose gay,
Starts, the new voice of Spring to hear,
    And imitates thy lay.

What time the pea puts on the bloom,
    Thou fli'st thy vocal vale,
An annual guest in other lands,
    Another Spring to hail.

Sweet bird ; thy bower is ever green,
    Thy sky is ever clear ;
Thou hast no sorrow in thy song,
    No winter in thy year !

Oh could I fly, I'd fly with thee !
    We'd make, with joyful wing,
Our annual visit o'er the globe,
        Companions of the Spring.
                        *John Logan.*

♣    ♣    ♣

## TIBBIE SHIEL'S.

This famous inn still stands by St. Mary's Loch in Yarrow, and the visitor may still sit in the kitchen that has sheltered Scott, Wilson, Hogg, Wordsworth, and many another bard. Hogg's cottage, Mountbenger, is only two miles down the glen. The original Tibbie was a Mrs. Richardson.

A cosy bield, sirs, this o' Tibbie's—just like a bit wren's nest. A wren's nest's round and theekit wi' moss—sae is Tibbie's ; a wren's nest has a wee bit canny hole in the side o't for the birdies to hap in and out o', aiblins wi' a hangin' leaf to hide and fend by way o' door— and sae has Tibbie's ; a wren's nest's aye dry on the inside, through drappin' on the out wi' dew or rain—and sae is Tibbie's ; a wren's nest's for ordinar biggit in a retired spat, yet within hearin o' the hum o' men, as weel's o' water, be it linn or lake—and sae is Tibbie's ; a wren's nest's no easy fund, yet when you happen to keek on't, you wunner hoo ye never saw the happy house afore—and sae is't wi' Tibbie's ; therefore, sirs, for sic reasons, and a thousand mair, I observed, " a cosy bield this o' Tibbie's —just like a bit wren's nest."

*Christopher North : " Noctes Ambrosianæ."*

♣     ♣     ♣

## THE BEAUTIFUL CITY OF GLASGOW.

Though that poor, half-witted bard, McGonagall of Dundee, died in 1902, he and his amazing doggerel remain legendary in Scotland—whether in virtue of the largeness of his ambition or of the unique badness of his verse, the reader of these characteristic stanzas may decide.

O, beautiful city of Glasgow, which stands on
    the river Clyde.
How happy should the people be which in ye
    reside :
Because it is the most enterprising city of the
    present day.
Whatever anybody else may say.

The ships which lie at the Broomielaw are
    most beautiful to see,
They are bigger and better than any in Dundee ;
Likewise the municipal buildings, most gor-
    geous to be seen,
Near to Ingram Street, not far from Glasgow
    Green.

O, wonderful city of Glasgow, with your triple
  expansion engines,
At the making of which your workmen get
  many singeins ;
Also the deepening of the Clyde, most mar-
  vellous to behold,
Which cost much money, be it told.

Then there is a grand picture gallery,
Which the keepers thereof are paid a very large
  salary ;
Therefore, citizens of Glasgow, do not fret or
  worry,
For there is nothing like it in Edinburgh.

O, beautiful city of Glasgow, I must conclude
  my lay,
By calling thee the greatest city of the present
  day :
For your treatment of me was by no means
  churlish,
Therefore, I say, " Let Glasgow Flourish."

*William M'Gonagall.*

♣        ♣        ♣

THE CURSE OF SCOTLAND.

The " Curse of Scotland " is a name given to
the nine of diamonds in a pack of cards.  It is
said to have originated from the tidings of a
severe defeat of the Scots having been written

on the back of this card. Grose, however, gives a different account of the reason of this singular designation:—

"The nine of diamonds; diamonds, it is said, imply royalty, being ornaments to the imperial crown; and every ninth King of Scotland had been observed, for many ages, to be a tyrant and a curse to that country. Others say it is from its similarity to the arms of Argyle; the Duke of Argyle having been very instrumental in bringing about the Union, which, by some Scottish patriots, has been considered as detrimental to their country."

*Hislop : " The Book of Scottish Anecdote."*

♣    ♣    ♣

## THE LORD'S PRAYER.

This rendering in old Scots is quoted by John Pinkerton in his " History of Scotland " (1797).

Uor fader quhilk beest i Hevin.
Hallowit weird thyne nam.
Cum thyne kinrik.
Be dune thyne wull as is i Hevin, sva po yerd.
Uor dailie breid gif us thilk day.
And forleit us uor skaths, as we forleit tham
    quha skath us.
And leed us na intil temtation.
Butan fre us fra evil.   Amen.

# THE STORY OF MACBETH.

It was on the following record, published in 1577, that Shakespeare based his tragedy.

Nocht lang after, happened ane uncouth and wonderful thing, by which followed soon a great alteration in the realme. By adventure, Makbeth and Banquho were passing to Fores, where King Duncane happened to be for the time, and met by the gait three women, clothed in strange and uncouth weed. They were judged, by the people, to be weird sisters. The first of them said to Makbeth, " Hale, Thane of Glammis ! " The second said, " Hale, Thane of Cawder ! " and the third said, " Hale, King of Scotland ! " Then said Banquho, " What women be ye, so unmercifull to me, and so favourable to my companion ? For ye give to him not only lands and great rents, but great lordships and kingdoms ; and give me nought." To this answered the first of the weird sisters : " We show more felicite appearing to thee than to him ; for though he happen to be a king, his empire shall end unhappily, and none of his blood shall after him succeed ; by contrary thou shalt never be king, but of thee shall come many kings, which with long progression shall rejoice the crown of Scotland." As soon as their words were said, they suddenly vanished out of sight. Makbeth, revolving all things as they were said by the weird sisters, began to covet the crown ; and yet he concluded to abide while he saw the time gaining thereto, firmly believing that the third weird should come, as the first two did before. But his wife, impatient of long tarry, as all women are (specially where they are desirous of any purpose), gave him great artation to pursue the third weird, that she might become ane Queen : calling him oft times febil coward, and not desirous of honours ; since he dared not assaile the thing with manhood and courage. Makbeth by persuasion of his wife, gathered his friends to a counsel at Innerness, where King Duncane happened to be for the time. And because he found sufficient opportunity, he slew King Duncane in the seventh year of his reign.

*Holinshed : " Chronicles."*

♣     ♣     ♣

## "LAND OF THE MOUNTAIN AND THE FLOOD."

O Caledonia ! stern and wild,
Meet nurse for a poetic child !
Land of brown heath and shaggy wood ;
Land of the mountain and the flood !
Land of my sires !     *Sir Walter Scott*

## SCANDAL IN DUNFERMLINE.

As Keats observed, the power of the Church in Scotland over the everyday affairs of the people used to be remarkably comprehensive. This is only a typical illustration of how the authority was used.

1646, 3rd May. That day, Robert Shortus and Katherine Hutsoun, his wyff, being convictit before the session of filthie slandering and abominable speeches against some lasses and virginis, viz., Janet Henderson, Katherine Cowan, Helen Nicoll, and Margaret Home, is ordainit, viz., the said Robert to mak his publick repentance therefore before the pulpit, and both he and his wyff to ask of the parties offendit foregiveness before their awin doores in the street, publicklie on their knees. And it is hereby actit and statute that if the said Robert shall be fund hereafter in the lyke fault, or in any other slander against his neighbours (he being of tymes found scandalous before), either in word or deed, that he shall be banished out of the paroche.

*Dunfermline Kirk Session Records.*

♣     ♣     ♣

## THE BALLAD OF CAPTAIN KIDD.

Scotland produced at least one of the most notorious of pirates, Captain William Kidd, born the son of a minister at Greenock. The scapegoat of his aristocratic employers,

155

he was hanged at Wapping in 1701. A popular ballad of the time, of which a few verses are printed below, calls him Robert.

My name was Robert Kidd, when I sailed,
    when I sailed,
  My name was Robert Kidd when I sailed,
      My name was Robert Kidd,
      God's laws I did forbid,
And so wickedly I did, when I sailed.

My parents taught me well, when I sailed, when
    I sailed,
  My parents taught me well, when I sailed,
      My parents taught me well,
      To shun the gates of hell,
But 'gainst them I rebelled, when I sailed.

I'd a Bible in my hand, when I sailed, when I
    sailed.
  I'd a Bible in my hand, when I sailed,
      I'd a Bible in my hand,
      By my Father's great command,
And I sunk it in the sand, when I sailed.

I murdered William Moore, as I sailed, as I
    sailed,
  I murdered William Moore, as I sailed,
      I murdered William Moore,
      And laid him in his gore,
Not many leagues from shore, as I sailed.

To Execution Dock, I must go, I must go,
  To Execution Dock I must go,
      To Execution Dock,
      Will many thousands flock,
But I must bear the shock, and must die.

Come all ye young, and old, see me die, see me
    die,
  Come all ye young and old, see me die,
      Come all ye young and old,
      You're welcome to my gold,
For by it I've lost my soul, and must die.

Take warning now by me, for I must die, for I
    must die,
  Take warning now by me, for I must die,
      Take warning now by me,
      And shun bad company,
Lest you come to hell with me, for I die.

*From a Broadsheet.*

    🕭    🕭    🕭

## AN EDINBURGH ASSEMBLY.

Oliver Goldsmith, when a poor student at Edinburgh University, visited one of the fashionable gatherings or "assemblies," and left this caustic description of "high life" in the Scottish capital in the eighteenth century :—

When the stranger enters the dancing-room he sees one end of the room taken up by ladies, who sit dismally in a group by themselves, and at the other end stand their pensive partners that are to be. The ladies may ogle and the gentlemen may sigh, but an embargo is laid upon any close converse. At length the lady directress pitches upon a gentleman and a lady to minuet, which they perform with a formality approaching to despondency. After five or six couples have thus walked the gauntlet, all stand for the country dance, each gentleman furnished with a partner from the aforesaid lady directress. So they dance much and say nothing, and this concludes an assembly.

*Oliver Goldsmith in a letter.*

♣ ♣ ♣ ♦

**THE MIST ON TINTO.**

Tinto, or Tintock, is a prominent hill in the upper ward of Lanarkshire.

On Tintock tap there is a mist,
And in that mist there is a kist,
And in that kist there is a caup,
And in that caup there is a drap.
Take up the caup and drink the drap,
And set the caup on Tintock tap.

*Traditional.*

## SISTER NATIONS.

I am quite certain that all our success with Scotland has been due to the fact that we have in spirit treated it as a nation. I am quite certain that Ireland is a nation ; I am quite certain that nationality is the key to Ireland ; I am quite certain that all our failure in Ireland arose from the fact that we would not in spirit treat it as a nation. It would be difficult to find, even among the innumerable examples that exist, a stronger example of the immensely superior importance of sentiment to what is called practicality than this case of the two sister nations. It is not that we have encouraged a Scotchman to be rich ; it is not that we have encouraged a Scotchman to be active ; it is not that we have encouraged a Scotchman to be free. It is that we have quite definitely encouraged a Scotchman to be Scotch.

*G. K. Chesterton : " All Things Considered."*

♣      ♣      ♣

## THE NEUTRAL.

Sir Michael Malcolm of Loch Orr, an eccentric baronet, wrote these lines when troubled with talk of the French Revolution.. Benarty is a hill which looks down on Loch Orr :—

Happy is the man who belongs to no party
But sits in his ain house and looks at Benarty.

## TASTES IN FISH.

One of the minor mysteries of creation is the great superiority of the haddock—the opposition " fish of St. Peter "—in Scotland over the same fish caught south of Tweed and Solway. I do not mean " yellow " " Finnan " or " Findon " haddocks—most patriotic Scots have, to my surprise, told me that the best of these are smoked in the east of London—but the actual ordinary " white fish." They are hardly eatable with us, while, whether " crappit-head "-ed or plain, or in the curious mixture called " fish-and-sauce," they are excellent up there. On the other hand, " white pollack," which is capital eating when caught in the Channel, is scorned, I believe, and justly so, as " lythe " by the Caledonian stern and wild.

*George Saintsbury : " A Last Scrap Book."*

❧ ❧ ❧

## SABBATH OBSERVANCE.

This anecdote relates to a period so recent as the first half of the nineteenth century.

On first going to Ross-shire to visit and preach for my excellent friend Mr. Carment, of Rosskeen, I asked him on the Saturday evening before retiring to rest, whether I would get warm water in the morning ? Whereupon he held up a warning hand, saying, " Whisht, whisht ! " On my looking and expressing astonishment, he said with a twinkle in his eye, " Speak of shaving on the Lord's day in Ross-shire, and you need never preach here more ! " In that same county Sir Kenneth Mackenzie directed my attention to a servant girl, who, if not less scrupulous, was more logical in her practice. She astonished her master, one of Sir Kenneth's tenants, by refusing to feed the cows on the Sabbath. She was ready to milk but would by no means feed them ; and her defence shows that though a fanatic, she was not a fool. " The cows," she said—drawing a nice metaphysical distinction between what are not and what are works of necessity and mercy that would have done honour to a casuist— " The cows canna milk themselves, so to milk them is a clear work of necessity and mercy ; but let them out to the fields, and they'll feed themselves."

*The Rev Thomas Guthrie : " Autobio-graphy."*

♣     ♣     ♣

**TULLOCHGORUM.**

Burns called this " the best Scotch song Scotland ever saw." Certainly the breezy stanzas of the Rev. John Skinner, the Episcopal clergyman of Longside, near Peter-

L

head, are not beaten for jollity by anything in Scots.
They have all the lilt of reel-music in their lines.  Skinner's
inspiration is said to have been a foolish quarrel between
Whigs and Jacobites of a house party.

Come gie's a sang, Montgomery cried,
And lay your disputes all aside ;
What signifies't for folks to chide
    For what's been done before them ?
Let Whig and Tory all agree,
Whig and Tory, Whig and Tory,
Let Whig and Tory all agree
To drop their Whigmegmorum.
Let Whig and Tory all agree
To spend this night with mirth and glee,
And cheerful sing alang wi' me
    The reel of Tullochgorum.

O, Tullochgorum's my delight ;
It gars us a' in ane unite ;
And ony sumph that keeps up spite,
    In conscience I abhor him.
Blithe and merry we's be a',
Blithe and merry, blithe and merry,
Blithe and merry we's be a',
    And mak a cheerfu' quorum.
Blithe and merry we's be a',
As lang as we hae breath to draw,
And dance, till we be like to fa',
    The reel of Tullochgorum.

There need nae be sae great a fraise
Wi' dringing dull Italian lays ;
I wadna gie our ain strathspeys
    For half a hunder score o' 'em.
They're dowf and dowie at the best,
Dowf and dowie, dowf and dowie,
They're dowf and dowie at the best,
    Wi' a' their variorum.
They're dowf and dowie at the best,
Their allegros, and a' the rest,
They canna please a Scottish taste,
    Compared wi' Tullochgorum. . . .

*John Skinner.*

♣     ♣     ♣

## THE SCOTTISH BALLADS.

There is no more delightful reading in
the world than these Scottish ballads. The
mailed knight, the Border peel, the moonlight
raid, the lady at her bower window—all these
have disappeared from the actual world, and lead
existence now as songs. Verses and snatches of
these ballads are continually haunting and
twittering about my memory, as in summer the
swallows haunt and twitter about the eaves of
my dwelling. I know them so well, and they
meet a mortal man's experience so fully, that I
am sure—with, perhaps a little help from

Shakespeare—I could conduct the whole of my business by quotation—do all its love-making, pay all its tavern scores, quarrel and make friends again in their words, far better than I could in my own. If you know these ballads, you will find that they mirror perfectly your every mood. If you are weary and down-hearted, behold, a verse starts to your memory trembling with the very sigh you have heaved. If you are merry, a stanza is dancing to the tune of your own mirth. If you love, be you ever so much a Romeo, here is the finest language for your using. If you hate, here are words which are daggers. If you like battle, here for two hundred years have trumpets been blowing and banners flapping. If you are dying, plentiful are the broken words here which have hovered on failing lips.

*Alexander Smith : " Dreamthorp."*

♣      ♣      ♣

**AN AMAZON OF 1733.**

I had never seen such a virago as Lady Bridekirk, not even among the oyster-women of Prestonpans. She was like a sergeant of foot in women's clothes ; or rather like an over-grown coachman of a Quaker persuasion. On our peremptory refusal to alight, she darted into the house like a hogshead down a slope, and returned instantly with a pint bottle of brandy—a Scots pint, I mean—and a stray beer-glass, into which she filled almost a bumper. After a long grace said by Mr. Jardine—for it was his turn now, being the third brandy-bottle we had seen since we left Lochmaben—she emptied it to our healths, and made the gentlemen follow her example : she said she would spare me as I was so young, but ordered a maid to bring a gingerbread cake from the cupboard, a luncheon of which she put in my pocket. This lady was famous, even in the Annandale border, both at the bowl and in battle : she could drink a Scots pint of brandy with ease ; and when the men grew obstreperous in their cups, she could either put them out of doors, or to bed, as she found most convenient.

*Alexander Carlyle : " Autobiography."*

      ♣     ♣     ♣

SCOTTISH WAR CRIES:—

The King of Scots—*St. Andrew !*
Douglas—*A Douglas ; a Douglas !*
The Gordons—*Gordon, Gordon, Bydand !*
The Earls of Winton—*Set on !*
Jedburgh—*Jethart's here !*
The Grants—*Stand Fast, Craigellachie !*
The Earl of Home—*A Home, a Home !*

## OSSIAN'S ADDRESS TO THE SUN.

This brief extract is from the most famous passage of a once famous poem, now one of the curiosities of literature. There is an indisputable eloquence in this rhythmic prose, but the twentieth century will probably be content to dip and smile, where the eighteenth memorized and doted— in spite of Dr. Johnson's doubts of Macpherson's honesty.

O, thou that rollest above, round as the shield of my fathers ! Whence are thy beams, O sun ! thy everlasting light ? Thou comest forth in thy awful beauty ; the stars hide themselves in the sky ; the moon, cold and pale, sinks in the western wave ; but thou thyself movest alone. Who can be a companion of thy course ? The oaks of the mountains fall ; the mountains themselves decay with years ; the ocean shrinks and grows again ; the moon herself is lost in heaven, but thou art for ever the same, rejoicing in the brightness of thy course. When the world is dark with tempests, when thunder rolls and lightning flies, thou lookest in thy beauty from the clouds, and laughest at the storm. But to Ossian thou lookest in vain, for he beholds thy beams no more ; whether thy yellow hair flows on the eastern clouds, or thou tremblest at the gates of the west. But thou art perhaps like me, for a season ; thy years will have an end. Thou shalt sleep in thy clouds, careless of the voice of the morning.  Exult, then, O sun, in the strength of thy youth !  Age is dark and un-lovely ;  it is like the glimmering light of the moon when it shines through broken clouds, and the mist is on the hills ;  the blast of the north is on the plain ;  the traveller shrinks in the midst of his journey.

*James Macpherson : " Ossian."*

&clubs;        &clubs;        &clubs;

## A GRAPHIC PERORATION.

This remarkable specimen of pulpit eloquence is quoted by Hislop in his " Book of Scottish Anecdote."

The Rev. A— C—, of D—, in discoursing of a certain class of persons who were obnoxious to him, concluded with this singular peroration :

" My freens, it is as impossible for a sinner to enter the kingdom o' heaven, as for a coo to climb up a tree wi' her tail foremost and harry a craw's nest ;  or for a soo to sit on the tap o' a thistle and whistle like a laverock."

&clubs;        &clubs;        &clubs;

## "THE BEGGAR'S OPERA" IN GLASGOW.

Towards the close of this moneth (August, 1728) a company of Strollers and Comedians came to Glasgou, part of A. Ashton's people at Edinburgh, to act the Beggar's Opera.  The Magistrates wer applyed to for a room, and

Bailay Murdoch, who is too easy, as is said, by a mistake gave a kind of allouance of the Weighouse to act in. They acted two or three dayes, and had very feu except the first day, After that they got not so much as to pay their music.

*Robert Wodrow : " Memoirs."*

♣ ♣ ♣

### THE TWO SCOTS.

Every Scotchman is two Scotchmen. As his land has the wild, barren, stern crags and mountain peaks, around which tempests blow, and also the smiling valleys below, where the wild-rose, the foxglove, and the bluebell blossom, so the Scotchman, with his rugged force and hard intellect in his head above, has a heart below capable of being touched to the finest issues. Sentimental, enthusiastic, the traces of a hare-brained race floating about him from his Celtic blood, which gives him fire, he is the most poetic being alive. Poetry and song are a part of his very nature. He is born to such a heritage of poetry and song and romance as the child of no other land enjoys. Touch his head, and he will bargain and argue with you to the last. Touch his heart, and he falls upon your breast. . . .

*Andrew Carnegie.*

## HAPPY DAYS.

At the king's return every paroche hade a minister, every village hade a school, every family almost had a Bible, yea, in most of the countrey all the children of age could read the Scriptures. . . . Every minister was a very full professor of the reformed religion, . . . was obliedged to preach thrice a-week, to lecture and catechise once, besides other private duties wherein they abounded. . . . I have lived many years in a paroche where I never heard ane oath, and you might have ridde many miles before you hade heard any ; Also, you could not for a great part of the countrey have lodged in a family where the Lord was not worshipped by reading, singing, and publick prayer. No body complained more of our church government than our taverners, whose ordinary lamentation was, their trade was broke, people were become so sober.

> *James Kirton* (1620—1699) *: " Secret and True History."*

     ♣     ♣     ♣

## SOUP IN SCOTLAND.

Cocky Leeky is a soup made of fowl with leeks, to which an alliance with a piece of beef is very advisable ; the leeks are very little

shorn, so as to make it difficult to eat it without
offence against delicacy by some slobbering. I
remember an English gentleman who was men-
tioning a dinner he had got in Edinburgh in
which tho' the soup was excellent he could not
recollect its name. " But it was a soup," said he,
" of which a mouthful was one half in the
mouth, and the other half out."

> *Henry Mackenzie : " Anecdotes and
> Egotisms."*

&#9827;   &#9827;   &#9827;

## MARTYRDOM IN THE NORTH.

The internal dissensions of the Presbyterian Church are
too complicated for the understanding of the alien. Sec-
tarian differences, however, have provided Scottish novelists
with an inexhaustible store of humorous material. No
writer has more adroitly exploited the possibilities of the
subject than Sir James Barrie, whose banter, in this
case, does not exaggerate the bitterness of denominational
feeling.

" Ay, weel," said the U.P., rising, " we'll see
how Rob wears—and how your minister wears
too. I wouldna like to sit in a kirk whar they
daurna sing a paraphrase."

" The Psalms of David," retorted Whamond,
" mount straight to heaven, but your para-
phrases sticks to the ceiling o' the kirk."

" You're a bigoted set, Tammas Whamond,
but I tell you this, and it's my last words to you

the nicht, the day'll come when you'll hae Mr. Duthie, ay, and even the U.P. minister, preaching in the Auld Licht kirk."

"And let this be my last words to you," replied the precentor, furiously ; "that rather than see a U.P. preaching in the Auld Licht kirk I would burn in hell fire for ever ! "

*J. M. Barrie : "The Little Minister."*

♣ ♣ ♣

**THE LAST OF SIR WALTER.**

The length of this quotation is justified by its beauty and dramatic interest. Here the end of Scott, a great Scotsman, is greatly recorded.

At a very early hour on the morning of Wednesday the 11th, we again placed him in his carriage, and he lay in the same torpid state during the first two stages on the road to Tweedside. But as we descended the vale of the Gala he began to gaze about him, and by degrees it was obvious that he was recognising the features of that familiar landscape. Presently he murmured a name or two—" Gala Water, surely— Buckholm—Torwoodlee." As we rounded the hill at Ladhope, and the outline of the Eildons burst on him, he became greatly excited ; and when, turning himself on the couch, his eye caught at length his own towers at the distance of a mile, he sprang up with a cry of delight.

The river being in flood, we had to go round a few miles by Melrose bridge ; and during the time this occupied, his woods and house being within prospect, it required occasionally both Dr. Watson's strength and mine, in addition to Nicolson's, to keep him in the carriage. After passing the bridge, the road for a couple of miles loses sight of Abbotsford, and he relapsed into his stupor ; but on gaining the bank immediately above it, his excitement became again ungovernable.

Mr. Laidlaw was waiting at the porch, and assisted us in lifting him into the dining-room where his bed had been prepared. He sat bewildered for a few moments, and then resting his eye on Laidlaw, said—" Ha ! Willie Laidlaw ! O man, how often have I thought of you ! " By this time his dogs had assembled about his chair—they began to fawn upon him and lick his hands, and he alternately sobbed and smiled over them, until sleep oppressed him. . . .

On Monday he remained in bed, and seemed extremely feeble ; but after breakfast on Tuesday the 17th he appeared revived somewhat, and was again wheeled about on the turf. Presently he fell asleep in his chair, and after dozing for perhaps half an hour, started awake and shaking the plaids we had put about him from off his shoulders, said—" This is sad idleness. I shall forget what I have been thinking of, if I don't set it down now. Take me into my own room, and fetch the keys of my desk." He repeated this so earnestly that we could not refuse ; his daughters went into his study, opened his writing-desk, and laid paper and pens in the usual order, and I then moved him through the hall and into the spot where he had always been accustomed to work. When the chair was placed at the desk, and he found himself in the old position, he smiled and thanked us, and said —" Now give me my pen, and leave me for a little to myself." Sophia put the pen into his hand, and he endeavoured to close his fingers upon it, but they refused their office—it dropped on the paper. He sank back among his pillows, silent tears rolling down his cheeks, but composing himself by and by, motioned to me to wheel him out of doors again. Laidlaw met us at the porch, and took his turn of the chair. Sir Walter, after a little while, again dropped into slumber. When he was awaking, Laidlaw said to me—" Sir Walter has had a little repose." " No, Willie," said he—" no repose for Sir Walter but in the grave." The tears again rushed from his eyes. " Friends," said he,

" don't let me expose myself—get me to bed—that's the only place." . . .

As I was dressing on the morning of Monday the 17th of September, Nicolson came into my room, and told me that his master had awoke in a state of composure and consciousness, and wished to see me immediately. I found him entirely himself, though in the last extreme of feebleness. His eye was clear and calm—every trace of the wild fire of delirium extinguished. "Lockhart," he said, "I may have but a minute to speak to you. My dear, be a good man—be virtuous—be religious—be a good man. Nothing else will give you any comfort when you come to lie here." He paused, and I said—"Shall I send for Sophia and Anne?" "No," said he, "don't disturb them. Poor souls! I know they were up all night—God bless you all." With this he sunk into a very tranquil sleep, and, indeed, he scarcely afterwards gave any sign of consciousness, except for an instant on the arrival of his sons.

They, on learning that the scene was about to close, obtained anew leave of absence from their posts, and both reached Abbotsford on the 19th. About half-past one p.m. on the 21st of September, Sir Walter breathed his last, in the presence of all his children. It was a beautiful day—so warm, that every window was wide open—and so perfectly still that the sound of all others most delicious to his ear, the gentle ripple of the Tweed over its pebbles, was distinctly audible as we knelt around the bed, and his eldest son kissed and closed his eyes. No sculptor ever modelled a more majestic image of repose.

*J. G. Lockhart : " Life of Scott."*

♣     ♣     ♣

**PROUD CHIEFTAINS.**

" A great hero was Clanranald," said the old folk. " He would have seven casks of the ruddy wine of Spain in his stable, and if a stranger asked what that was for he would be told that that was the drink for Clanranald's horses. And when the hero would go to London he would make his smith shoe his horse with a gold shoe, and only one nail in it ; and the horse would cast the shoe in the great street, and the English lords would gather round about it and pick it up and say : ' Sure the great Clanranald is in London—here is a golden shoe.' "

One of the Macneill chiefs, however, went one better than that. Each evening after dinner he sent a trumpeter up to his castle-tower to make the following proclamation : " Ye kings, princes, and potentates of all the earth, be it known unto you that Macneill of Barra has dined —the rest of the world may dine now ! "

> *Kenneth Macleod : In his Notes to "Songs of the Hebrides."*

♣    ♣    ♣

## A LADY OF THE OLD SCHOOL.

Edinburgh as the capital of Scotland, has had its masters and mistresses of mode. In his "Memorials of his Time," Henry Cockburn has left us a delightful portrait of a *grande dame* of the old school—Mrs. Rochead of Inverleith.

Except Mrs. Siddons in some of her displays of magnificent royalty, nobody could sit down like the Lady of Inverleith. She would sail like a ship from Tarshish, gorgeous in velvet or rustling silk, done up in all the accompaniments of fans, earrings and finger-rings, falling sleeves, scent-bottle, embroidered bag, hoop, and train ; managing all this seemingly heavy rigging with as much ease as a full-blown swan does its plumage. She would take possession of the centre of a large sofa, and at the same moment, without the slightest visible exertion, cover the whole of it with her bravery, the graceful folds seeming to lay themselves over it, like summer waves. The descent from her carriage, too, where she sat like a nautilus in its shell, was a display which no one in these days could accomplish or even fancy. The mulberry-coloured coach, apparently not too large for what it contained, though she alone was in it ; the handsome, jolly coachman and his splendid hammer-cloth loaded with lace ; the two respectful liveried footmen, one on each side of the richly carpeted step—these were lost sight of amidst the slow majesty with which the Lady of Inverleith came down and touched the earth.

*Henry Cockburn : " Memorials of his Time."*

&clubs; &clubs; &clubs;

BURNS *v.* BURNS.

" Read the exquisite songs of Burns," Tennyson exclaimed, " in shape each of them has the perfection of the berry ; in light the radiance of a dewdrop ! You forget for its sake those stupid things, his serious pieces." The same day I met Wordsworth and named Burns to him. Wordsworth praised him even more vehemently than Tennyson had done, as the great genius who had brought poetry back to Nature, but ended : " Of course I refer to his serious efforts, such as the ' Cotter's Saturday Night ' ; these hollow little songs of his one has to forget." I told the tale to Henry Taylor that evening ; but his answer was : " Burns's exquisite songs and Burns's serious efforts are to me alike tedious and disagreeable reading."

*Aubrey de Vere : " Memoir of Tennyson."*

♣    ♣    ♣

## THE SINGING OF " AULD LANG SYNE."

Heavy feeding, a careless collocation of guests, dull and rambling speeches, bad singing, an inferior piano, a poor accompanist, and a negligent chairman have their fitting culmination in a mumbled and mangled rendering of Burns's immortal Song of Friendship. The dragging tune, the self-conscious stare, the fish-like hand extended to the trusty " friend " (*sic*), the ghastly galvanism of the prestissimo, proclaim the feast a fiasco. The end is all. Let us get " Auld Lang Syne " right and make the feast lead up to it. Let us get it into our noddles that there are no " days of auld lang syne " in the song ; that " And surely ye'll be your pint-stowp, And surely I'll be mine," means " You'll pay for one pint and I'll pay for another " (treat about or no treating) ; that " dine " means noon ; that the last verse begins, " And there's a hand (not ' haun '), my trusty fiere," fiere meaning crony ; and that " a right gude-willy waught " means a right full-of-goodwill long draught. Finally, let us

follow the example of the 'fifty-niners and
entrust each of the first four stanzas to one of
four picked and reliable vocalists, and the last
stanza to the four vocalists singing in parts,
reserving our united energies for the recurrent
and final chorus and the breaking-off " three
cheers." Fortune gave us the greatest of the
world's song-writers, who gave the world its
best convivial songs. Why not show ourselves
worthy of the honour ?

*William Power : " Robert Burns and
Other Essays."*

♣ ♣ ♣

## AULD LANG SYNE.

It is fitting that this collection should close with the
national parting-song. The verses, indeed, are so often
misquoted or mumbled that the convivial may welcome the
authentic version of the ballad. The actual phrase, " Auld
Lang Syne," is proverbial and was used as the burden of an
artifical ballad printed in James Watson's Collection, 1711.
Here are two verses of that early effusion :—

Should old acquaintance be forgot,
　　And never thought upon,
The flames of love extinguished,
　　And freely past and gone ?
Is thy kind heart now grown so cold
　　In that loving breast of thine,
That thou canst never once reflect
　　On old long syne ?

Where are thy protestations,
    Thy vows, and oaths, my dear,
Thou mad'st to me and I to thee,
    In register yet clear ?
Is faith and truth so violate
    To th' immortal gods divine,
That thou canst never once reflect
    On old long syne ?

Allan Ramsay was taken with the idea and sought to improve on the older song. He failed conspicuously as this verse shows :

Methinks, around us, on each bough,
    A thousand Cupids play ;
Whilst through the groves I walk with you,
    Each object makes me gay.
Since your return the sun and moon
    With brighter beams do shine,
Streams murmur soft notes while they run,
    As they did lang syne.

It was left to the genius of Robert Burns to take the old idea and produce the inimitable song that has found a place in the hearts of all Scotsmen—and in the hearts of many members of less fortunate races.

Should auld acquaintance be forgot,
    And never brought to min' ?
Should auld acquaintance be forgot,
    And auld lang syne ?

For auld lang syne, my dear,
    For auld lang syne,
We'll tak' a cup o' kindness, yet,
    For auld lang syne.

We twa ha'e run about the braes,
    And pu'd the gowans fine ;
But we've wander'd mony a weary foot
    Sin' auld lang syne.

We twa ha'e paidled i' the burn,
    From morning sun till dine ;
But seas between us braid ha'e roar'd
    Sin' auld lang syne.

And there's a hand, my trusty fiere,
    And gie's a hand o' thine ;
And we'll tak' a right guid-willie waught,
    For auld lang syne.

And surely ye'll be your pint-stowp,
    And surely I'll be mine ;
And we'll tak' a cup o' kindness yet,
    For auld lang syne.

*Robert Burns.*

♣     ♣     ♣

# GLOSSARY

Aboon, *above.*
Ahint, *behind.*
Airn, *iron.*
Bairn, *child.*
Bandster, *binder of sheaves.*
Bauk, *cross-beam.*
Bield, *shelter.*
Bigg, *to build.*
Biggin, *building.*
Birk, *birch.*
Blad, *fragment.*
Bucht, *cattle-fold or sheep-pen.*
Ca', *to drive, convey.*
Caller, *fresh.*
Canny, *cautious.*
Cantrip; cantraip, *trick.*
Chandler-chaftit, *lantern-jawed.*
Cheekie for chow, *side by side.*
Cheep, *chirp.*
Chiel, *fellow.*
Corbie, *raven, crow.*
Coup, *upset.*
Crack, *to converse : conversation.*
Craig, *rock.*
Cramasie, *crimson cloth.*

Creel, *perplexity*.
Crine, *shrivel*.
Crouse, *confident*.
Cushie, *cushat-dove*.
Daffing, *joking*.
Daud, *lump*.
Dine, *noon*.
Ding, *knock*.
Dominie, *schoolmaster*.
Doo, *dove*.
Dowf, *dull*.
Dowie, *sad*.
Driech, *dreary*.
Dub, *puddle*.
Dule, *sorrow*.
Fail dyke, *turf wall*.
Fail sunk, *turf seat*.
Fash, *to anger*.
Fashious, *vexatious*.
Faught, *struggle*.
Fleech, *to beguile*.
Gab, *impertinent talk*.
Gait ; gate, *way ; road*.
Gar, *to make : to cause*.
Geisened, *leaking*.
Glower, *scowl*.
Gowan, *daisy*.
Greet ; grat, *to weep : wept*.
Gyte, *mad*.
Hecht, *promised : offered*.
Hoast, *cough*.
Hott, *heap*.
Houlet, *owl*.

Howk, *to dig.*
Hulie and fear, *cautiously and quietly.*
Hure, *whore.*
Ilka, *each.*
Jaud, *jade.*
Jimp, *neat.*
Joup, *skirt ; petticoat.*
Kaim, *comb.*
Keek, *to look.*
Land-loupin', *land-stealing.*
Lane, *alone.*
Lang syne, *long ago.*
Lave, *the rest.*
Laverock, *lark.*
Leal, *faithful.*
Lee-lang, *livelong.*
Leglen, *milk-pail.*
Lichtlie, *disparage.*
Lirk, *fold.*
Loaning, *milking-park.*
Lowe, *light : flame.*
Lown, *serene.*
Lug, *ear.*
Lum, *chimney.*
Lyart, *hoary.*
Mane, *moan.*
Mear, *mare.*
Mickle, *much.*
Minny, *mother.*
Neb, *nose.*
Nick-ñackets, *frivolities.*
Opensteek hems, *ornamental edges.*
Oxter, *armpit.*

Paitrick, *partridge.*
Pickle, *a little.*
Pownie, *pony.*
Preen, *a pin : to pin.*
Quaigh, *drinking-cup.*
Rax, *to pass : hand.*
Rug, *to pull.*
Sea-maw, *seagull.*
Sheugh, *ditch.*
Sklent, *to slant.*
Smoor, *to suffocate ; drown.*
Snood, *hair-band.*
Sough, *sigh.*
Souple, *supple.*
Speer ; speir, *to ask.*
Spelder, *to sprawl.*
Stieve, *substantial.*
Stoorie, *active.*
Stoup, *measure : pail.*
Stoure, *dust : strife.*
Stoussie, *healthy child.*
Sturt, *trouble.*
Sumph, *stupid fellow.*
Theek, *to thatch.*
Thraw, *to twist.*
Thrums, *threads.*
Tirl, *knock.*
Touzie, *rough, untidy.*
Truff, *turf.*
Twine, *to part : separate.*
Wae, *sad.*
Wame, *stomach.*
Waukrife, *wakeful.*

Wede, *vanished*.
Weirdless, *ill-fated : worthless*.
Whigmaleerie, *gimcrack*.
Whin; whinne, *gorse*.
Winnock-bunker, *window-seat*.
Yowe, *ewe*.

# INDEX
*to authors, titles, subjects,
and first lines of poems*